C H I W I D

Other books in the Transmontanus series

1   A GHOST IN THE WATER   *Terry Glavin*

3   THE GREEN SHADOW   *Andrew Struthers*

4   ALL POSSIBLE WORLDS   *Justine Brown*

5   HIGH SLACK   *Judith Williams*

6   RED LAREDO BOOTS   *Theresa Kishkan*

7   A VOICE GREAT WITHIN US   *Charles Lillard with Terry Glavin*

8   GUILTY OF EVERYTHING   *John Armstrong*

9   KOKANEE: THE REDFISH AND

THE KOOTENAY BIOREGION   *Don Gayton*

10   THE CEDAR SURF   *Grant Shilling*

11   DYNAMITE STORIES   *Judith Williams*

12   THE OLD RED SHIRT   *Yvonne Mearns Klan*

13   MARIA MAHOI OF THE ISLANDS   *Jean Barman*

14   BASKING SHARKS   *Scott Wallace and Brian Gisborne*

15   CLAM GARDENS   *Judith Williams*

16   WRECK BEACH   *Carellin Brooks*

17   STRANGER WYCOTT'S PLACE   *John Schreiber*

TRANSMONTANUS   2

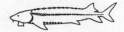

Published by New Star Books
Series Editor: Terry Glavin

CHIWID

Collected by

Sage Birchwater

TRANSMONTANUS / NEW STAR BOOKS VANCOUVER

Ulkatcho

Nazko

Quesnel

Dean R

Fraser River

Hwy 20

Anahim Lake

to Bella Coola

Nimpo Lake

Chilcotin R

Chezacut

Towdystan

Alexis Cr

Charlotte Lake

Chilanko Cr

Puntzi Lake

Redstone

Alexis Creek

Williams Lak

Clearwater Lake

Kleena Kleene

Tatla Lake

Chilanko Forks

Anaham Reserve

Riske Cr

Pyper Lake

Tatla Lake

Stone

Hwy 20

One Eye Lake

Eagle Lake

Chilko R

Toosey

Hanceville

Cochin Lake [Kwatzine]

Choelquoit [Big Eagle] Lake

Chilcotin R

Tatloyoko Lake

Henry's Crossing

Mosley Cr [West Branch]

POTATO MOUNTAINS

Fraser River

Klinaklini R

C O A S T

Homathko R

Nemiah Valley

Chilko Lake

M O U N T A I N S

Knight

Bute

Inlet

Inlet

0   20   40   60   80 km

0 10 20 30 40 50 mi

Contents

The Country Was Still Raw   9

All the Cold Winters   17

Potato Mountain   29

Priest Time   41

Loozap   47

Faults on Both Sides   55

To Have a Witchdoctor Sing With Granny   63

After He Went Crazy   75

Fire on Top of the Ice   91

I Take Him From Coyote   103

Stone Rancherie   113

Acknowledgements   125

THE COUNTRY
WAS STILL RAW

The country in those times was changing. It was still an unbroken sea of jackpine and spruce forests that rose from the Fraser River and spread westward to the rugged peaks of the Coast Mountain Range, some 320 kilometres away. But it was a time of great hardship and sorrow for the Tsilhqot'in people. Sickness and disease had weakened them and reduced their numbers. Newcomers were making their way into the high Chilcotin Plateau country, a territory the size of Vancouver Island. Some came on foot, others by saddlehorse, others still by covered wagon.

On June 18, 1904, the Oblate priest, Father François Marie Thomas, sprinkled water on the head of a child not quite a year old, and said her name: Lillie Skinner. It was "priest time" at Redstone Flats, deep in the heart of Tsilhqot'in territory.

FACING PAGE: *Crossing the Taseko River into the Nemiah Valley in a big-wheel wagon.*

In those times, the Catholic Church was starting to have its way with the Tsilhqot'in people. Many Tsilhqot'in, too, were eager to learn more of the whiteman's ways, so as not to be at a disadvantage in their dealings with the outside world. Churches were being built at several villages throughout the territory occupied by the nomadic Tsilhqot'in. The annual event known as priest time served the Tsilhqot'in as instruction in whiteman lore.

Father Thomas was making his annual trek through the country. His journey began some three or four weeks earlier in the Blackwater country to the north. Once there was enough green grass for feed, he set out by saddle horse from Quesnel to the Southern Carrier village of Nazko. From there he continued west to Kluskus, then on to Ulkatcho Village. Turning south, he followed the Dean River to Anahim Lake, where he was met by a delegation of Tsilhqot'in who brought him east into their homeland.

At Redstone Flats, the Tsilhqot'in people gathered from distant camps in the surrounding countryside to receive their yearly sacraments from the priest. Marriages were conducted, graves were blessed, and babies were officially welcomed into the Church. This backlog of the previous year's Church business was attended to in less than a week's time.

It was for these reasons that in 1904, the young mother, Loozap, had camped at Redstone with the infant daughter she named Chiwid. The child had been born shortly after the priest's last visit to the country the previous June.

Chiwid was baptized Lillie Skinner on account of two problems the Canadian government and the Church encountered among people whose custom was to own just a single name. The government wanted a register of the Tsilhqot'in people, and it needed a census so that reserve lands could be set aside and the land could be laid open for preemption and settlement by the whiteman. The other problem was that the Tsilhqot'in names, spoken in the language of the country, were often unintelligible to non-Tsilhqot'in speakers. In their official record-keeping, then, the Church bestowed English names on their Tsilhqot'in converts. A first and last name, in the manner of the British and European tradition.

This was all new to Loozap as she approached Father Thomas. And to complicate matters further, the young mother was born deaf and could only speak "on her hands."

As she stood before the altar with her child, it was somehow communicated to the priest that the child's father was a whiteman, Charlie Skinner, who ranged herds of horses in the country to the south. He had preempted a vast string of meadows in the shadow of the Potato Mountains.

Father Thomas filled out the baptismal record as follows: "Lillie (Skinner), age 11 months, Redstone Flat, B.C., June 18, 1904."

Beside "father's name," the record was left blank. Beside "mother's name," the record reads: "Lausap (Rosa)." Loozap received the comfort of an English name as well.

As for the infant girl, she would go on to a life that confounded both Tsilhqot'in and whiteman. Many people called her "half crazy and half coyote." Others felt that at some point in her life, her human spirit had departed and that the spirit of an animal had taken its place.

I first passed through the Chilcotin country in the spring of 1973. I was hitchhiking to Bella Coola, and the country was still raw then. It still had that mark of innocence that is always there when the balance between the natural forces and mankind is tilted noticeably on nature's side. The road between Williams Lake and Bella Coola was narrow and unpaved, and it undulated with each contour of the land. Many people still relied upon a rubber-wheeled wagon drawn by a team of horses. I encountered several of these outfits along the highway as I made my way westward.

Beyond the highway in the broad network of wild-grass meadows, people still cut hay using horse-drawn mowers and rakes, and piled it in towering stacks using derrick poles. Many families spent the winters in these remote places feeding their horses and few head of cattle, and perhaps setting a few traps in the winter time. People lived close to the land and their life was governed by the seasons, the weather, and the condition of the road. On the whole, the people were independent and self-reliant. They made their living as best they could, scratching out an existence as opportunity provided. What the country lacked in economic opportunity and natural wealth it made up for in other ways. There was a richness of character and a preponderance of unique individuals.

The land was steeped in tradition that lingered as if caught in a back-eddy of time. While the rest of the world watched astronauts landing on the moon, life in the Chilcotin continued as it had for decades. Slow and easy, and not all that concerned with what lay beyond the natural boundary of the Fraser River.

And in the hills, not far from where I passed that spring day 22 years ago, a Tsilhqot'in woman sat by her tiny fire, even less concerned about the outside world than her neighbours were. Her name was Chiwid, and she had just survived another long winter in the high plateau country.

I never did meet Chiwid. But after travelling to Bella Coola and returning to Williams Lake, it seemed clear that my fate would bring me back to the Chilcotin. I could not deny the extent to which this rugged and mysterious country moved me. The Chilcotin represented the ultimate in wildness and freedom. Unconquered country. Untamed, untamable. So, within a few weeks, I moved to Williams Lake, and soon I began hearing stories about Chiwid.

In 1977, I moved out to Tatla Lake and began living among some of the legendary personalities who carved their existence out of this isolated landscape. I ran a trapline and took up journalism, writing about the Chilcotin for the Williams Lake *Tribune* and *Coast Mountain News* of Bella Coola. I got the chance to meet more of the characters of the Chilcotin, and I began recording their stories.

Some of these stories were about Chiwid. Not pretty stories, some of them, but through these reminiscences of Chiwid, a common theme was woven. Stories about Chiwid became a story about the Chilcotin, of events experienced by the people who lived there. It was a story about the transformation of a country, the clash and integration of cultures, and the strength of individuals.

This book is a collection of these accounts.

— Sage Birchwater

Chiwid holding her grand-
daughter Irene Lulua at
Choelquoit Lake, 1950s. The
cabin, in a large meadow
known as Henry's Meadow on
the west end of Choelquoit
Lake, belonged to Henry Lulua
and Chiwid's daughter Mary
Jane.

There was a couple of feet of snow on the ground, but no fire, no nothing. No sign of life. They were just about to go when the snow cracked in front of them. Chiwid pushed the snow off her blanket, and stood up. There was one log laying there, and she was laying down beside it, buried under the snow.

—CHARLIE QUILT

She was singing one time. She thinking just like a coyote.

Maybe her body's just like something. Some kind of old animal. That's why she do that. She just think of something. Must be like that. She thinks she's a coyote. That's how she stays warm.

— EUPHRASIA WILLIAM

God damn, she was a beautiful woman then. Hard to believe . . . Damn, she was a good looking woman. One of those people who didn't have to do anything. She's just good looking. She could have been all mud and dirt out of the gutter, and she was still good looking. You see the odd person like that, and she was one of them. — RANDOLPH MULVAHILL

One time, in late fall, people were hearing some strange noises above Tatla Lake, and people called in the authorities . . . The locals were laughing about it. All they ever found was old Chiwid's camp. It sounded like a cougar screaming or a wolf howling, they said. — MARTY MOORE

Chiwid was a very beautiful woman when I first came into this country in 1940. I remember seeing her camped in a little grove of poplar trees at Graveyard Springs, along the old road into the West Branch. I remember how beautiful she was. All by herself, with very beautiful, long black hair, as shiny as a raven's wing. She was just there in the wilderness. — GERRY BRACEWELL

The name comes from the sound the bird makes. In January, it goes "chee-wit." In February, "chee-chee-wit," and in March it goes "chee-chee-chee-wit." — HANK LAW

She always used little strings to catch animals. She lived outside and survived. The elders told us kids to stay away from Granny. They said she was really bad because she got spiritual powers. Even my Aunt Jenny said she had bad spiritual powers. — RITA LULUA MELDRUM

ALL THE COLD
WINTERS

GRACE KELLOGG *moved to the Chilcotin with her husband to run the Kleena Kleene Lodge on One Eye Lake in 1953. They stayed at the lodge five years before selling out and moving to Tatla Lake. Her husband worked for the Graham Ranch while Grace worked in the store.*

I saw her once in a while.

One time when our daughter, Carol, was riding her horse to Puntzi, she was very late in arriving, so we became concerned and went out looking for her. We saw this little fire way off in this meadow, and went over to it, and saw Chiwid sitting there all hunched up. But we didn't really talk to her. I think she indicated she hadn't seen anybody.

Then another time, Betty and I went out. It was pretty early winter, and Betty had been real concerned about her. So we went out and

FACING PAGE: *Donald Ekks.*

Chiwid 17

found her. I don't remember where it was, but it was way out in the woods some place. And she had built this lean-to – very well built, out of branches – into a kind of teepee effect. And she had a little fire in there. Just a small fire.

So she came with us quite willingly, and we brought her to a little cabin, up the hill a little ways from the big ranch house in Tatla Lake. I guess she stayed there maybe one or two nights. And then she left.

I remember every time I ever saw her, she had on lots of clothes. Maybe three or four skirts and petticoats, and usually moccasins. Even in the cold winter time. She wore those old-fashioned rubbers over her moccasins. In the winter they were just frozen hard. She'd come into the store and her feet would clatter over the floor.

The thing I really remember about her was that she was always kind of happy looking.

FRANK CHUNDEE *found refuge in Nemiah Valley after leaving the United States during the 1960s to avoid the military draft. Frank was given the name "Chundee," which means "jackpine" in Tsilhqot'in, by Henry Solomon of Nemiah Valley. After more than two decades in the valley, Frank continues to live close to the land, gathering much of what he needs to live on. He goes barefoot from spring until fall and makes several walking trips over the mountains each year to Lillooet to visit friends and gather mountain potatoes, berries and other fruit.*

I first heard of Chiwid from Henry Solomon in Nemiah Valley. He related my lifestyle to hers. Maybe because I was camping out and also because I was into gathering. I just gathered sticks and I had a saw. It was a little bit different. Also the fact that she had given up Alec Jack and I was single. That's how I knew about Chiwid, from Henry.

The only thing worth telling is a little story about seeing her walking up the road out of Stone. I remember right where she was, too. She was on the left-hand side of the road, walking up toward Nemiah. And she had her stick, too. Right away I knew it was Chiwid and I told the guy who was driving to stop the truck, because I had to do something for Chiwid. I wasn't quite sure what it was going to be, but I had to make some sort of communication there.

So I got out and got into the back of the truck and figured I should give her something. Then I rummaged around trying to figure out what I should give her. We had some dried fruit. So I thought, well, I'll try that. That'll be something maybe.

So Chiwid was standing there, and I guess she could figure out that I had something to give her. She could sort of feel that out. So then I handed her a fig. And I remember she held that fig up and said: "Fig!" That was really nice the way she did that.

Anyway, the only other thing was that when I looked at her face, it was a glowing face. I'd never seen a face like that before or since.

That's about all I have to say about it. That was the end of it. I got back in the truck and away we went. That was the end of it. I suppose when I used to come back in camp I'd think about Chiwid, although I knew she was out of this world compared to the way I was living, certainly no comparison to what I was doing and what she was doing.

That's why I never went to visit her. Henry was telling me I should go visit her. But I could never impose on anybody who was living like that. I never would have felt right about it. If you're living like that, you're living as a spirit. You're not living as a body. If you're living like a body you're not going to be able to live like that.

DON FADENRECHT *was a Chilcotin guide-outfitter, trapper and fur buyer for 20 years from the mid-1960s to the mid-1980s. He moved to Puntzi Lake in 1966, where he and his wife Mildred owned and ran the Puntzi Lake Resort.*

In the early 1960s, we were coming to visit my father-in-law Cliff Southwood, who started the resort on Puntzi Lake in 1952. On the way, we stopped to speak to an elderly Indian lady, camped under a spruce tree. She had a small fire going and she was roasting a grouse. Cliff told me at that time that her name was Lillie Skinner, and that she never went indoors anywhere. She spent the entire year outside.

I met her one or two times during those years when I was buying fur from the native people. I once met her at the old Chilanko Store that was being operated by Mrs. Wilson and her son, Ross. I bought a few squirrel skins from her. Another time I was directed to a house to buy some fur, and she was there. I recognized her, but I had no further dealings with her as far as I remember . . .

Some of her relatives came to see her at various times and tried to get her to come in out of the bush. But apparently she just adamantly refused. She didn't want to be indoors anywhere. She just wouldn't go. I think she had pretty poor eyesight at the time that I knew her. She would really squint even if you were standing about five feet away from her. As if she was trying to recognize who you were. She must have been quite a woodswoman, because she looked after herself out there. She apparently snared grouse and shot the odd squirrel.

The squirrels I bought from her were shot. So she must have still been able to shoot then. But I would guess she would have had to get very close to her targets. Also, obviously she used a lot of fish. I've heard people say she netted fish at the mouth of creeks at various times.

It was amazing how she moved around. One time you'd hear of her being somewhere up Nimpo Lake way. The next time you'd hear of her being somewhere down at Fletcher Lake [Big Creek] and that country. Then up farther up into Nemiah and places like that. She seemed to really get around.

FRED ENGEBRETSON (1909–1989) *was a descendent of Norwegian colonists who arrived in Bella Coola via Minnesota in 1894. Fred's father, Thomas Engebretson, and grandfather, Jakob Lunos, established the Engebretson Ranch in 1901 at a spot known as Towdystan, where the trail forked east along the Chilanko River and south to the Klinaklini. Eventually, the main highway took the southerly route and the Chilanko Trail was abandoned.*

She hunted squirrels. I guess she made the odd dollar selling the skins. She'd have a little net in the creek and catch suckers and trout. Yeah, she lived off the land. She was a little bit loose in the head, but she could survive. People must have been amazed at that. Especially when she didn't freeze to death. Because she hardly had any camp outfit. Everything was on her saddlehorse . . . grub, and whatever she slept in. All she had was a tarp . . . no tent. She might have had one, but she never put it up.

In them days squirrels were worth more than they are now. She was pretty good at shooting squirrels . . .

She didn't talk to any white people. Maybe now and then if she wanted something.

Morton Casperson, she talked to him one day here. She said: "One boy kill a moose." And she pointed that way. "Well maybe that way." And she pointed in four directions. She must have just dreamed it.

The Indians liked Morton Casperson, because he was a lot of fun. She'd talk to him. But this made no sense.

He lived like the Indians. He'd stay wherever he could find a place. One time she was camped over the hill here, and I went down the road with Morton Casperson. We had a team and wagon and two dogs ran ahead of us. When we got to her camp, Lillie climbed a tree. She looked like a bear going up the tree. She must have been scared of the dogs, although she must have seen those dogs for weeks.

Lillie never caused any trouble, she never stole anything.

She was good at surviving cold spells. She didn't like it in a warm house. "Too warm," she'd say.

Chiwid just had a .22 single-shot. But she was wondering where she could get a .25/.20 because she thought by this time, that the .22 was a little bit too small to kill a moose, although she did kill a moose with it. She gave me some of the meat.

DORIS LULUA, *born in 1930, is the eldest daughter of Eleene Lulua and Bob Pyper. She has lived all her life in the Eagle Lake*

area between Tatlayoko Valley and the Chilko River. She owns a
small ranch with her brother Casimile and sister Madeline.

My sister Madeline she like'em for Lillie. She was friend. She want
him, you know. My sister, she said Lillie had peanuts, candies, cook-
ies. She said, "Lillie feed me lots. And he cook pretty good."

Lillie fishing for kokanee at Eagle Lake, and she had a camp down
there. Lillie make a long net for my sister too, one year. Make net out
of Number 10 thread. And my sister she make for him one.

Lillie good shot with .22. Her rifle got no sight on it. She lost the
sight. You know that pine gum? Well, she chew it up and she make'em
sight. Sure funny looking that one. And she shoot with it for deer. She
kill deer. Sometimes she shoot for moose too. She's good shot. And
she shoot muskrat and squirrel. Her eyes were good at one time. Shoot
anything.

ALEX MATHESON *rode a freight train from Ontario to British*
Columbia in 1935 and eventually came to the Chilcotin in 1940.
He worked at the Chilco Ranch feeding cattle for eight months to
earn enough money to buy two mares and a colt. From there, he con-
tinued westward to Tatla Lake on horseback. "Coming out this side
of Redstone, I remember you could reach out either side of the sad-
dle horse and pick willow twigs off the brush." Alex took up land at
Cochin Lake on the road to Tatlayoko Valley.

I first met her on the road near Tatla Lake. She was travelling with
two horses. She had a pack on one, and a saddle on the other. We
were going across Tatla Lake Flats, which was all corduroyed to keep
the trucks from settling in the mud.

Chiwid was quite friendly looking. A little old girl, with a big smile.
I always spoke to her, and stopped to have a few words when I saw her.
She used to have several head of cattle, which she kept up towards
Anahim Lake. That's why they called her the Cattle Queen. Most of
the other Indians didn't have any cattle.

According to what I heard, she kept a few hundred dollars on her most of the time. I guess she got a cheque. A bit of a pension. But I think she ate about as much as a canary. Whenever I went by her camp, it didn't look like she hardly had anything around her.

She would be sitting out in a meadow with a little fire, making tea. I think she drank barrels of tea.

You'd see her all over the place. At one time you were apt to see her up towards Anahim Lake. Another time she'd be camped down here along the Tatlayoko Road. Then you'd see her down at Chilanko, or over at Chilko. Always camped off the road. She travelled all over, but she never hung around people.

When it was cold, it didn't look like she had enough clothes any time I saw her. I don't know what she had in her pack, though. She might have had lots of clothing. She was a tough old girl to take that cold. Nobody else stayed out any longer than they had to. When it was really cold, people felt sorry for her and had her come in their house. But she couldn't stand it. She had to get back out and live her usual life, camping out all the time.

Somebody told me she went sort of crazy if she got in the house. She couldn't stand it. She had to have air.

EDNA DOWLING *married Stan Dowling in 1940, and moved with him to Anahim Lake. Stan was well established in the Chilcotin with a store and trucking business. Then in 1942 they bought the Kleena Kleene Ranch from Pat McClinchie, and moved there in 1944.*

Chiwid used to pass by the ranch on her way to Tatla Lake to buy her groceries, or to go stay with her brother Scotty at Clearwater Lake. Not with him, but she camped nearby.

She stayed between Tatla Lake and Anahim Lake, just camping along, all winter long. Everyone was so amazed how she could live through all the cold winters and the snow.

She always went through our place because it was a shortcut, up through our field to Kleena Kleene on the righthand side of One Eye

Lake. I never got to talk to her about anything, because she didn't want to talk. I tried to talk to her. She would kind of smile and go through, but she wouldn't stop and talk. She always had four or five horses, but she never rode. She'd be leading her horse and had the colts from three other horses following along. She always had her little pack on her back as well, and seemed very happy.

At night when she slept she'd dig into the ground and make a little fire, which heated the ground. Then she'd take out all the ashes, and that's where she slept.

She'd look at you, and was always so afraid. Her eyes would look at you as if you were going to hurt her or something. She wouldn't let you get close.

DONALD EKKS *was born in 1923 at Clearwater Lake just west of Kleena Kleene. For years he trapped, hunted and worked on ranches between Kleena Kleene and Redstone. Today, he lives with his wife Emily Lulua near Tatla Lake. They continue to live in the traditional manner of the Tsilhqot'in people, moving with the season to various camps throughout their traditional territory.*

Chiwid kind of funny. Lay down any place, no fire, sleep all day. Sometime never move. And he get up in the night time. Sit down, eat'em, cook'em fish.

Kind of funny. He don't want to stay with you. He stay out. Tell him, Come in. He don't want to come in. Just little while, I guess.

And cold. Tell him come inside all winter. No, he don't want to. He stay over there. I don't know. Funny. Maybe he don't like the house. Too warm, I guess.

Yeah, he just don't like the house. He try and put'em the wood in the stove. Pretty near burn the house one time. Maybe that's why he scared. He come in and he just keep putting wood in the fire. He burn his roof, pretty near. He do that down at Chilko Lake.

He go in the house. Just like he shake. You know, cold. Outside he pretty good. Sure funny.

MARTY MOORE, *grandson of K.B. Moore who started the Circle X Ranch, and son of guide-outfitter Gerry Bracewell. Marty was raised in Tatlayoko Valley and he continues to trap and hunt as the time permits.*

In the mid-60s, I remember Chiwid camped on the west side of the road halfway between Tatlayoko and Tatla Lake. There was no water there, but that didn't seem to bother her.

She'd disappear for a month or two, then show up every once in a while in a place like this. There was a campfire, a bucket and a tub and all her bundles that she packed around. She'd be there for maybe a couple of weeks.

Ken Haynes would say, in the early 60s, that woman had the sharpest eyes of anyone he ever met. He'd give her a ride, and she'd see squirrels and chickens [grouse] on the edge of the road. She'd get all excited.

One time, in late fall, people were hearing some strange noises above Tatla Lake, and people called in the authorities. They got the troops in from Puntzi, and they hiked all around. The locals were laughing about it. All they ever found was old Chiwid's camp. It sounded like a cougar screaming or a wolf howling, they said.

GERRY BRACEWELL *came to Tatlayoko Valley from Alberta in 1940 to work for K.B. Moore, her future father-in-law. She took over the ranch after K.B. died in the 1950s. She is a registered big game guide and is well known for her knowledge of the outdoors and wilderness.*

Chiwid was a very beautiful woman when I first came into this country in 1940. I remember seeing her camped in a little grove of poplar trees at Graveyard Springs, along the old road into the West Branch. I remember how beautiful she was. All by herself, with very beautiful, long black hair, as shiny as a raven's wing. She was just there in the wilderness.

That's when I started becoming interested in her activities, because nobody knew much about her. There were stories that went around that her husband mistreated her, that she was a bit demented as a result of the mistreatment. Because he was jealous.

She had a saddle horse, but the last one she had died at Barr Hill. Fred Linder saw Lillie walking with a tobacco can of water, trying to revive her dead horse. Fred told her that the horse was dead. That she couldn't bring it back to life.

She was known as the Cattle Queen to the Graham family. Eventually she lost all her cattle.

One time Fred and Betty [Linder] heard a weird sound up in the hills on a very cold winter night. It was 40 below and Fred and Betty went to investigate it. They found Lillie's camp. She had a very small fire, and was camped there with just one miserable little blanket. They felt sorry for her, and Betty managed to get a small pension for her, so she could have food. She wouldn't even use it to benefit herself by it. Her family used it.

People were totally amazed at her endurance. She was very wise as far as wilderness goes . . .

I remember her catching fish on the north end of Potato Mountain. There's a little pond up there and a little creek trickles through it and there's a swamp lake. She had a little rock dam on the creek, then she'd let the water out. The fish would get stranded in the dry creek bed and she'd go along and pick them up.

Marvin Baptiste tells a story about Chiwid when she was camped at Choelquoit Lake one time. She caught a bunch of fish and cooked them in the big pot she used to pack around. She set the pot off the campfire to cool down, then decided to take a little nap. Asleep on her blanket, she was awakened by this old smacking and slopping going on. She opened her eyes and there was a big black bear with his head in the pot, eating all her trout. She leaped up over the fire and kicked the bear in the butt. The bear took off without looking back to see what was chasing it.

Lillie had a lot of guts. She wasn't afraid of anything.

ALF BRACEWELL *is a long-time rancher and sawmiller in Tatlayo-ko Valley. In 1953, Alf drove one of the two bulldozers which opened the road between Bella Coola and the rest of the province.*

Chiwid wasn't outgoing. She was like most of the old Indians . . . especially the women. You'd say hello . . . and then they'd kind of say hello and smile . . . and that was the end of the conversation.

Unless you got somebody like Eleene [Lulua]. She'd talk both your ears off you.

POTATO

MOUNTAIN

LOU HAYNES *came to Tatlayoko Valley with his mother and four brothers in 1929 when he was 14 years old. His mother, Del Naomi Haynes, became the local postmistress. Lou spent many years exploring the Chilcotin on horseback, making his living hunting wild horses, cowboying, ranching, trapping and guide-outfitting.*

The old Indians didn't like to live in houses. In the winter they'd stay in a cabin, but as soon as it was warm enough in the spring, they'd move out and stay in a tent. They'd camp all year until late fall. They didn't like to have children born in a house. When the time came, the woman would pack up and go out and build a fire. She'd tie a pole between two trees, something she could hang on to, and have the child outside.

Most of the Chilcotin Indians had a little meadow where they

FACING PAGE:
The Haynes brothers of Tatlayoko, 1935: Ken, Laurie, Ray, Lou and Harry.

could cut a little hay and winter their horses. They all had a few head of cattle.

In late winter, they all migrated toward their trapping grounds to go hunting muskrat and beaver and whatever they could find. They'd start out with a team and sleigh, and would have the parts of a wagon in the sleigh. In spring, as the snow melted, they'd put the parts of the wagon together and come out that way. They'd stop at the store at Tatla Lake and trade what fur they had, and go on home.

In July, they'd all migrate out and head for Potato Mountain. Wagon load after wagon load, saddle horses and pack horses all tied on behind. Some herded along. They'd go up there and spend about a month. The women would dig potatoes and the men would hunt deer and hold horse races.

Everyone from Redstone would be there. They would come down Tatlayoko Valley and would take their wagons as far up the hill as they could. They'd leave all the harness and stuff on the wagons, and go the rest of the way up the hill with saddle horses and pack horses.

Nobody would touch their stuff. They'd leave all the old people too feeble to ride up the hill on horseback at the camp with the wagons. I remember one old blind woman at the camp. They had pieces of ·buckskin string all tied together so she could find her way outside.

A woman could dig 50 pounds of those little potatoes in a day. They used an old broken rake tooth from a dump rake. They'd straighten it out and put a T-handle on it.

The Indians all made their own living in those days. They'd contract hay cutting, build fences, they had a few head of cattle. They were self-sufficient and independent.

CASIMILE LULUA *was born at Choelquoit Lake in 1927. His mother, Eleene Lulua, was the daughter of Jack Lulua, said to have been an eyewitness to the Chilcotin War of 1864. Casimile worked for years at Tatla Lake Ranch, then later as a cowboy for C1 Ranch of Alexis Creek. Today, he and his sisters Doris and Madeline own a small ranch near Henry's Crossing along the Chilko River.*

We used to dig potatoes up on Potato Mountain. Used to be we went up around the first of July. The end of June. Everybody went up there. Nobody'd go to the rodeo. People from Nemiah Valley, some from Redstone and Anahim Lake. Everybody went up there and so he camp.

Everywhere you look, somebody's camp. Dig some potatoes, shoot the deer, and eat some deer. Now everybody go to the rodeo. Then go to the next rodeo . . . and go to the next rodeo. Pretty soon it's fall time.

Lots of people went up to Potato Mountain. No bridge over Chilko River. Nemiah Valley people just go across with canoe. Make a canoe and swim his horses right across the river. And they left the canoe this side. When he go back, he take canoe. Take all his horse and swim them back the same way. Eagle Lake Henry used a big-wheel wagon to go across the river. He had lots of good, strong workhorses.

Everybody would take them mountain spuds. Take them off the mountain and make them dry. Then they keep them all winter. When you want to eat them, make them soaked. Keep them one night in the water, then cook it.

When we were digging potatoes, that's all we eat. Lots of guys hunt deer then too. Eat deer meat and potatoes.

HARRY HAYNES, *born in 1913, is the oldest of Del Naomi Haynes' five sons. He has lived most of his life in Tatlayoko Valley, ranching and guiding. He looked after his mother for many years and today he is "story-teller-in-residence" in Tatlayoko Valley. His wife, Fran, runs the post office.*

In 1928 or 1929, when I first came to the Chilcotin, the Indians would come along in Bennett wagons all heading for the Potato Mountains. Some came from Anahim Lake, some came from Redstone, some came from Nemiah Valley.

They'd all come along with these Bennett wagons just absolutely loaded. They usually had a couple of kids. A couple would be riding saddlehorse, driving some free horses. They'd come down through the valley and they'd go way up the sidehill, just as far as they could get up the creek.

The men would go hunting and they'd get two or three deer. In two or three days they'd get a real bellyfull of deer meat. Then they would take all the horses and pack them, and take everything they owned right to the top of Potato Mountain. Old Eagle Lake Henry and a whole bunch of other Indians from Nemiah Valley would come up from the other end, and they would all meet up on top there.

Oh God, would they have a ball. A big party. A rodeo with race horses.

ALEX MATHESON *saw all the traffic along the lonely stretch of road from Redstone to Tatlayoko Valley because the road used to pass through the centre of his ranch. He was always on friendly terms with the native people.*

I never went up there myself, but they used to come by my place in a big gypsy convoy of wagons and horses. Whole families would go up there. All the old Indians and kids. Kids would be riding all alone on a saddle horse following a wagon. Often they weren't much higher than the saddlehorn itself.

Down in Tatlayoko where Hesch lives today, they would make camp. They'd transfer everything from the wagons to packhorses, and head up the side of the mountain. They'd take some kind of sharp iron with them to dig the mountain potatoes with.

I ate some once. I was riding down to Redstone from Chilko Lake on a saddle horse, and passed Eagle Lake Henry's camp. He called me over and says, "Come and have supper with us." They were having mountain potatoes.

You know, as near as I can tell, they tasted like new potatoes.

Freshly dug and boiled. Mrs. Henry was reheating them and frying them. They tasted really good. That's the only time I got to taste them.

HAROLD ENGEBRETSON *was born in 1914 in Bella Coola, the second son of Thomas and Annie Engebretson. His brother Fred took up the family ranch at Towdystan, while Harold married Alice Holte and lived many years in Anahim Lake. He ranched and worked as a lineman for the Dominion Telegraph Company before retiring to Marguerite, on the Fraser River.*

During the 1920s and 1930s, the Indians were relatively well off. They were rich, better off than most of the whites. They worked and they trapped, and they all had a few cattle. They had lots of horses, and fur was worth a lot of money. They used to talk of one old Indian, old Capoose, who went to Vancouver with $25,000 worth of fur. That would be worth half a million today.

They were more independent. You see that with the white people today, too. People don't change actually. They become less independent. We are welfare people now. We want something for nothing.

ED SCHUK *moved out to Tatla Lake from Saskatchewan in 1936. After acquiring a few cows and some land at Lunch Lake along the Old Tatlayoko Road, he and his wife Helen took up ranching. Along with trapping and shooting squirrels for a cash income, Ed became one of the country's first registered game guides.*

In the spring, the Indians started arriving when the suckers started running in Cochin Lake. They came from Redstone with their teams and wagons, horses and dogs and whatever. Quite a few. Five or six wagons all together in a bunch. They camped right here at our place. That's why they call it Lunch Lake. Then they'd go on through and fish until the end of June, then go up the Potato Mountains.

The women would dig potatoes and the men would hunt the big bucks. They'd dry meat and dry potatoes until about August, then they'd come back off the mountains for hooshums [soapberries] and saskatoon berries. Then they'd split up and go cut hay for somebody or take a fencing contract. The Redstones went back to Siwash Bridge by salmon time, and a lot went back to Nemiah.

KATIE SCHUK *grew up in the Tatlayoko Valley where the trail leads up to the Potato Mountains. Today she and her husband Joe run a large ranching operation in Tatlayoko Valley and range their cattle in the Potato Mountains.*

They usually had a bone or a stick to dig the potatoes with, and a flour sack to put them in. It was June or July when they went up there, and they were there most of July. They would have lots of fun up in the mountains. A bunch would go hunting deer, the women would dig potatoes, and they would be fishing and having horse races. All kinds of goings-on.

When we were kids, we took the cattle up in the spring time. We'd meet the Indian pack horses coming up the trail. Lots of them some-times. We were with our parents coming home, and they'd be going up. We'd meet quite a few horses.

Most of the Indian women had a little papoose on their backs, a kid in front, and maybe one behind. Quite a few of the older kids rode dif-ferent horses. Maybe two or three on a horse. And a whole pack of dogs.

And then we'd get past all of that, and just as likely meet another bunch of them. We usually had a pack horse or two ourselves, and that takes up quite a bit of space. But we always managed to get past.

I saw Chiwid up there many years ago. I never talked to her, but talked to some of the others. Us kids never went up to see the rodeos. We just heard our dad telling about them. He would see them. We stayed pretty clear of there. We didn't really like all the noise, with their homebrew.

BUD MCLEAN *moved to the Chilcotin from Abbotsford in 1957. He and his wife bought the Chilko Lodge from Tom Garner. In*

Abbotsford they had a new house, a new car and four kids, some still in diapers, and Bud had a well-paying job with an oil company. "We junked it all, bought an old Dodge Powerwagon, and came up to the Chilcotin. It took twelve hours to come in from Alexis Creek, winching from tree to tree."

I remember the Indians going up and digging the wild potatoes. They often used to come and borrow my equipment. There'd be 20 of them, maybe 25. My little boy Larry, who is 32 years old now, used to go with them. They'd put him on top of the pack.

They'd go right up the trail to Fish Lake, where we take our trail rides today. I went there last year, and we come down into this valley, and the whole one side of that valley was white with potato blooms. Doris and Madeline Lulua still go up there. You see them come by here with their pack horses.

Years ago they used to take those square five-gallon oil cans, and they'd cut the tin out of the top. They'd go up with two on each side of the horse. Each horse would have four cans and they'd come back full of potatoes.

So, that was a big event. They'd have big races. A kind of sports day at a big flat between two lakes. It used to be a big deal, but now it's all gone. Nobody has the desire or patience. They'd be gathering stuff in the fall, just like the animals.

Really the glamorous old days. People have no idea anymore. A bloody caravan went in there.

WILF HODGSON (1918–1995) *was son of legendary Chilcotin truck-ing pioneer Tommy Hodgson, who began driving freight and mail to the Chilcotin from Williams Lake during the First World War. Wilf first travelled out to the Chilcotin with his father when he was a youngster during the 1920s. He finally took over his father's business with his brother, Cookie, after World War II. Later, Wilf and his wife, Drew, bought the Chilcotin Lodge at Riske Creek which they ran for several years during the 1960s and 1970s.*

You'd see the Indians camped all over the place in those days. Whole families coming along, up and down the road, with a team and covered wagon. Horses all tied on behind, and dogs. It was quite a sight.

First you'd see them coming to Williams Lake for the Stampede. Then they'd move back to the Chilcotin again, fishing and hunting all the way. Then they'd get back to their meadows and put up some hay.

For the Stampede, they'd come from all over the country, and it was quite a sight on the sidehill there. Tents, wagons and horses. All camped and the campfires going. Horses all tied up. Hobbles on and bells on. People don't realize what a sight that was. That was one of the main attractions of the Stampede. The Indians in those days had a lot of pretty good race horses.

Bob Pyper had a pretty big store down by Chilanko Forks. I stayed there overnight one time, with dad and this insurance salesman, and Arthur Haddock the fur-buyer. I was about 6 or 7 years old. It was Easter, in 1926, and the priest was coming.

It was a big get-together. Hundreds of Indians were coming to old Pyper's store, trading and bringing their furs in. There was all this excitement. Indians were coming from all directions with their pack horses and wagons.

I remember at night the Indians playing lahal. All night long you'd hear these Indians wailing away there. When you're a small kid, it kind of gives you an eerie feeling. I guess they had quite a bit of homebrew. By daylight in the morning it kind of quietened down. But I'll never forget that night.

Nobody came in cars. Father Thomas, the priest, came in a buggy. He travelled all over the country like that. You'd see the old joker anywhere.

I found old Bob Pyper dead in 1937. I had some mail and groceries for him. He lived at Pyper Lake, and was the only one between Redstone and Tatla Lake. I knocked at the door and he didn't answer. There was no smoke coming out of the chimney, so I went around and looked in the window. There he was staring at me, out the window. Then I realized he was dead.

So I had to get into his cabin to phone Andy Stewart at Redstone. It was winter time and he was frozen stiff.

LAURIE HAYNES *was nine years old when he and his four brothers arrived in Tatlayoko in 1929. The second youngest of Del Naomi Haynes' sons, he hayed for Andy Christensen in Anahim Lake in 1940 when he was 20 years old. "I did the wrangling and ran the hay rake with Pinky Christensen." Later he worked for Alfred Bryant, "packing grub" with a pack train from Bella Coola.*

I originally knew Chiwid at Eagle Lake when she was around with Tommy Lulua, George and Lashaway Lulua in 1933–34. Old Tommy used to come to my mother's house in Tatlayoko regularly, because she had the post office. He used to bring his Timothy Eaton catalogue and my mother would help him fill out his order.

Every summer, all the Indians used to come down to our place in Tatlayoko on their way to dig wild potatoes and hunt deer up on the Potato Mountains. They used to spend the summers with their teams and wagons and tents on the sidehills.

Old Tommy was the only Indian around Eagle Lake who had any cows. Every fall he'd put four or five in the main beef drive heading into Williams Lake from Tatlayoko.

When I first came to the country in 1929, there were very few of the Indians who could speak any English at all. Most of them lived 90 per cent the old way. The Indian way. It was pretty rough . . .

Old Jack Lulua, they called him Crazy Jack, because he was an individual. He was a long ways from crazy. Just like Chiwid, she was a long ways from crazy. He went his own way and did his own thing. And if anybody didn't like it, then they could kiss his ass. He had no idea where he came from or where his parents came from. He had no recollection of the early days and the life his parents lived, or whether he came from the Chilcotin. It didn't matter a bit to him.

One time up on Sunflower Hill when he was camped with Tommy Lulua and his bunch, he told me how when he was a young boy, that he went with the Indians that massacred old Waddington and his party down in the canyon. He told the whole story. How they waited until everybody went to work, then killed the cook and the flunky. Then killed the guys up on top of the canyon tending the ropes. Then cut all the ropes and pulled all the poles off the pins so the guys who were out there couldn't get back. Then dropped rocks on them until they killed them all.

LOUISA JEFF *was raised in the Riske Creek area by the Billy family.*

When I was a little girl I can remember going by horseback to Tatlayoko from Riske Creek to dig the wild potatoes. Lots of dik [saskatoon berries] too. Just saddlehorse can make it up to the top. Small trail. Wagons can't go up.

Mountain top, lots of wild potatoes. Dig them with just your finger. Little white flowers. You can see where they grow.

DORIS LULUA *was raised in the Eagle Lake country and is one of the few people who still goes up to the Potato Mountains in the early summer to dig the wild potatoes.*

Every year my mother went up Potato Mountain. One whole month each year. People just live on deer and potatoes. Them days no welfare. Government help nobody.

Every year my mom go up there. Every old people go up Potato Mountains. Make stampede. Had stampede grounds. Lots of fun. People camp everywhere. Mountain race. Lots of camp.

Now, not see very many deer. Last year, just see four or five. Before, lots of deer. All the Redstone people make lots of dry meat and dig lots of potatoes. Then come down. Go back home and start to make hay.

Lots of fun, Potato Mountain. Now too many cattle up there. In fall time hardly any grass. Just Huckleberry Mountain lots of feed for deer.

Them days, people not have much money. But they live real good.

Every Lulua lived around Chilko and Eagle Lake. Other side of Mountain House, lots of Indian people. Graveyards all over.

Learned about graveyards from old people. They tell you not to sleep on top. I know because my old gramma and grampa tell me, "You going to get sick if you sleep on top." Told me all about it.

Old Bapstick, my grampa, he's buried at Tsuniah Lake. North end. One guy build house right next to graveyard. My oldest brother Edward, he stay there. He said, "Old grampa never made any noise. Don't bother me. Went to Heaven long time ago."

DONALD EKKS *and his wife Emily live within view of the Potato Mountains at Cochin Lake where they set nets for suckers and trout. In August they go down to Henry's Crossing to catch and dry sockeye salmon. In winter they live in a cabin near Tatla Lake.*

We used to go up the Potato Mountains on horseback. On the old trail behind Harry Haynes' place. Come out at Chilko Lake by Tommy Lulua's. Had stampede up there. Sometime 25, 30 head of horse. Make'em horse race. All Redstone, Nemiah. Old Charlie West, P.L. West's granddad, come from Anahim Lake. Somebody bring homebrew.

I stay ten or twelve days. Look around the mountain. Dig at first mountain in middle of June. In July go to other mountain. All white flowers. Have a little iron. Sure lots of fun. My woman dig 50 pounds in one day. Long time ago.

DOREEN SEAFORTH *is Chiwid's oldest granddaughter, and is the oldest daughter of Julianna Setah and Willie George.*

Granny used to go to the Potato Mountains. She picked a lot of berries and dried them. The whole family used to go up for two weeks and dry some deer meat. Then we used to go back in the fall time to

Ellen Lulua, Henry Solomon, Minnie Lulua Charlieboy, and Lizzie Lulua.

hunt deer. Granny came with us. She'd be the first one to shoot the deer.

She used to go hunt squirrels in the winter time. Just about every day. All she had was a single-shot .22. All the white oldtimers knew her real well.

HENRY SOLOMON *was born at Toosey Reserve near Riske Creek, and was raised by his grandmother. When she was a child, she and her sister were the only survivers of a smallpox epidemic that hit her Tsilhqot'in village at Puntzi Lake. Today Henry and his wife Mabel live in Nemiah Valley surrounded by many of their children and grandchildren. They continue to live close to the land, ranching, trapping and hunting.*

Chiwid used to go up Potato Mountain to dig wild potatoes. Lots of Tsilhqot'in Indian up there.

Chiwid's husband, Alec Jack, he go to Potato Mountain, too. Some old people tell me story that Alec Jack used to make some kind of races. He look after that.

Those guys, they race. Bet money. Stake race. Four or five horses at one time. Just bet each other. Bet on anything.

Some good wrestler. Some guy from Anahim Peak, Stone. Some good boxer. Find out the best man in the whole Chilcotin. Race horses all that kind. Kind of a rodeo in the mountain.

PRIEST TIME

MACK SQUINAS *was born in Ulkatcho Village in 1923, some 50 miles north of Anahim Lake. His paternal grandfather, Domas Squinas, was once the only resident of Anahim Lake. Then, in the 1920s, white settlers began moving into the country, and during the 1930s and 40s many Ulkatcho families took up residence there as well.*

Once a year, every June, the priest came to Ulkatcho Village. He stay seven days. Once a year we see Father. Father Thomas was the first Father we see.

Lots of people went to Ulkatcho. All of Kluskus, some from Ootsa Lake, and some from Anahim Lake.

Then Father came to Anahim Lake. Stayed maybe one or two days. Then he go to Redstone. He used to ride saddle horse right from

Casimile Lulua, Lisa Hunlin,
Jeanie Lulua, and Dominique
Baptiste.

Nazko. Must be he rode saddlehorse all the way from Quesnel to Nazko, to Kluskus, to Ulkatcho, to Anahim Lake. Tsilhqot'in pick him up in Anahim Lake. Take him down to Redstone in a wagon.

Once a year, every June seventh, Father went through Ulkatcho Village. Lots of people get married. Lots get baptized.

JOHNNY BLATCHFORD *moved to Williams Lake in 1937 as a member of the Provincial Police Force. In 1940 he took the police posting in Alexis Creek, but left the force two years later because he didn't want to be transferred out of the area. While still in Williams Lake, Johnny arrested Eagle Lake Henry who had gotten a bit rowdy at the Stampede. Once he sobered up, Henry became very sorry for what had happened, and Johnny took a liking to him. The two men became lifelong friends. While still a policeman at Alexis Creek, Johnny broke horses in his spare time and traded them for cattle. By the time he left the Force he had a sizable herd and took up ranching at Tsuniah Lake, next door to Eagle Lake Henry.*

Father Thomas used to come out twice a year to hold mass and marry everybody. He was quite an old character. A real old Frenchman. He was still traveling out to the Chilcotin when I moved into the country.

Eagle Lake Henry said they couldn't convert him into the Catholic religion. He didn't believe the Catholic religion. He just held on to his old Indian religion.

He told me: "Is good enough. Just one Tyee anyway." That's what he figured. He said: "These Catholic can't fool me. I don't go for that."

He wouldn't let any of his kids be Catholics, either. He told me one time Father Thomas tried to screw his wife. She raised hell with him.

Henry used to always go to Redstone at priest time. One time, Father Thomas had brought a new priest out, and was introducing him around. Henry was sitting there gambling, playing cards, and

Mrs. Henry came crying to him. Her mother had died late that winter.

He said: "What's the matter with you Mrs. Henry?" He always called her Mrs. Henry.

She said: "Henry, I got to have $10. My mother died last winter and this new priest has prayed her through the first gate, but she's standing at the second one waiting to get in."

He said: "Mrs. Henry, you tell him to tell your mother to go to hell. The devil will take her for nothing."

IRENE BLISS *was born in a little log cabin down below Alexis Creek in 1913. She is a descendant of the Hance and Witte families of Hanceville, two of the original white families in the Chilcotin. She and her husband, Bill, still live at their Willow Springs Ranch, close to the confluence of the Chilcotin and Chilko Rivers between Redstone and Alexis Creek.*

There weren't many Indians living at Redstone Flats. They just used to come out there when the priest came.

Old Father Thomas, I remember him well. When I was young he always used to come visit us. We weren't Catholics, but he used to come and have lunch with us. He used to make his rounds twice a year. Once for the whites, and once for the Indians.

Oh, he was a wonderful man with a hearty laugh and a big white beard. Everybody knew him. He was known from one end of the country to the other. He went in all kinds of weather. It didn't matter what it was like, he'd go.

MARY ANN ROSS *was raised at Kleena Kleene by her mother Louise One Eye and her father George Turner. She ranched and looked after cattle all over the Chilcotin with her husband Jimmy Ross. Mary Ann's grandfather was Chief One Eye of One Eye Lake near Kleena Kleene. Her mother only had the use of one arm, but it is said she was more capable than most women with two. She tanned hides, trapped, rode saddle horse and did all that was expected of a woman living in the back-country. George is rumoured to have been an outlaw who drifted across the border from the United States in 1892 with a posse on his tail. It is said he never stopped running until he got to Bella Coola. He was thought to have been a member of the Dalton gang of train robbers. George was a man of great presence, a great trapper and outdoorsman. Turner Lake in Tweedsmuir Park is named after him.*

Big-wheel wagons, freight wagons. That's what they used to go down to Gang Ranch in the old days. Get a load of stuff all the way from Ashcroft. Put way high box on it.

That's the way they come and get together at priest time. The Indian all come out like that, with a big-wheel wagon. No car them days.

We come out just about that time from Kleena Kleene country. We stop too, maybe one day at priest time. We come out in a wagon like that too. That's the way they live in those days. They go across the river in a wagon like that too. Stuff piled up high.

Ev Wilson came to the Chilcotin in 1948. "We left Williams Lake at 7 a.m. and got to Alexis Creek by 10 at night. It took us five hours to get up Sheep Creek Hill from the Fraser River. It was spring breakup and the clay build-up on the wheels acted as brakes scraping on the truck box. We had to take axes, shovels or sticks and get the mud off the wheels." The photo shows Ev's daughter Diane in the Hodgson Brothers truck that brought them into the country.

L O O Z A P

DONALD EKKS' *first recollection of Chiwid was at Andy Stewart's store at Redstone when he was a young boy. Chiwid was there with her mother, Loozap.*

Chiwid was my first cousin. My dad, Charlie Ekks, was born in Bella Coola. Half like that. Half Bella Coola. He talk Bella Coola Indian language.

Long time ago, at Redstone Store, I see Chiwid and his mother. Call his mother Loozap. Him and Chiwid cook'em bacon. He don't need frying pan. Tell him, "Frying pan over there."

"No, we don't need it."

Just stick right there. Big slab of bacon. Cook right on fire. And just something on the bottom to catch the grease.

Loozap can't hear. Maybe half blind one side.

LUCY SULIN, *born in 1906, was only a few years younger than Chiwid. They grew up in the same part of the country. Lucy's mother was Louise One Eye and her father was a white man, George Dag. She was raised by her stepfather, George Turner, who, unlike many white men with native wives, treated Louise with great respect and caring.*

First time I see Chiwid, he was a young girl. Little bit older than me . . . At Clearwater Lake where they were trapping fish where the creek goes out of the lake.

I remember Chiwid's uncle, Little Johnny, looking for her. He had a big stick because Chiwid run off with some boys.

Little Johnny raised Chiwid. Her mother Loozap was deaf and couldn't speak.

ALICE ENGEBRETSON, *born in 1916, is the oldest child of Andy and Ada Holte who arrived in the Chilcotin in a covered wagon from Washington State in 1922. The Holte family, which also included Tommy (born in 1918) and Illa (born in 1920), took six years to work their way across the Chilcotin. They arrived at the Engebretson ranch house in Towdystan in 1927 and stayed there five years. This is where Alice first met Chiwid, her husband Alec Jack, and their two daughters Cecilia and Julianna. Chiwid's daughters were only slightly younger than the Holte children.*

Chiwid's father was a white man by the name of Charlie Skinner. I never knew him, but heard he was responsible for a lot of wild horses in the country. In Nemiah Valley. He acknowledged Chiwid as being his daughter, which is more than a lot of white men would do.

Chiwid's mother, Loozap, was deaf and dumb. She had lots of kids: Scotty Gregg, Ollie Nukalow, Madeline Palmantier, and a kid called Coyote Dag. All from different white fathers.

Coyote was a long, skinny guy, the thinnest man I've ever seen in my life. He died when he was 15 years old. The little fellow used to tag around with old Blind Seymour. He led the old man around by the hand and did all the chores for him. He died of TB that hard winter.

Scotty was Loozap's youngest child. He and his mother stayed with Chiwid and Alec Jack at Nimpo Lake, as long as the couple were together.

Everyone took in Loozap's children to raise.

TOMMY HOLTE (1918–1989), *the oldest son of Andy and Ada Holte, was four years old when his family arrived in the Chilcotin. They spent their first winter at Redstone, where his father fed cows for the Knoll Ranch. The next year they moved to Tatla Lake where the Holte children received their only schooling. Then they continued west to Kleena Kleene where Andy fed cattle for one winter, before arriving at the Engebretson ranch house at Towdystan.*

She was a nice looking woman.

Her dad was that fellow who used to raise horses in Nemiah Valley. Charlie Skinner. I never seen him, but heard lots about him. He was pretty well spoken of. He was supposed to have started the wild horses. I imagine he knew about Chiwid, I don't know.

Her mother was an Indian woman by the name of Loozap. It seems to me she couldn't talk. Ollie tried to talk to her with his hand, but he couldn't make it.

WILF HODGSON (1918–1995) *grew up in Williams Lake and made many freight runs to the Chilcotin from the 1920s to 1963.*

I remember old Charlie Skinner. He was supposed to be Chiwid's father.

He seemed to be everywhere in the country. Big Creek, Eagle Lake . . . somebody told me he had 500 head of horses on the Eagle Lake range.

He finally came to Williams Lake and lived the last few years of his life in the old Song Lee Hotel, located where the Lakeview Hotel parking lot is today.

He was a nice old man.

Louise One Eye Turner, 1952

As a provincial policeman in Williams Lake, it was part of JOHNNY BLATCHFORD's *job to help people fill out official papers and sign documents, so he got to know everybody who lived in the community and surrounding countryside pretty well.*

I first came to Williams Lake as a provincial policeman in November of 1937.

I knew Charlie Skinner real well. He was putting in his last days at a Chinese place called the Greasy Spoon, where the Lakeview Hotel parking lot is today. It was owned by Song Lee. Charlie and some other oldtimers lived upstairs and Song Lee fed them.

Charlie never mentioned having a daughter Chiwid. He had no use for Indians. He hated what he called "siwashes."

"God damn Siwashes," he said. "They're no good."

TOM CHIGNELL (1902–1994) *came to the Chilcotin in 1920 at the age of 17 to work for the Cotton Ranch at Riske Creek. His father was a medical doctor in England and his family never could understand his love for the rustic life in the Canadian wilds.*

I shared a cabin with Charlie Skinner once, when I was haying at Chilco Ranch. About 1925 or '26. He was getting up in age, in his mid 60s, and looked after the big percheron stallions. I was in my mid 20s. We did all the mowing for Chilco Ranch that summer. Two months straight without stopping. We each ran a mower.

Old Skinner was in the country quite a long time, no doubt about that. In the early 1920s, when I first came to the country, he had a good big bunch of horses around Eagle Lake. A couple or three hundred head. They simply ran loose. He brought good horses in. Good stallions, and he'd turn them loose and they'd run with the wild bunch.

He lived over at Kwatzine Lake. The railway was going to come through, and he built a big stopping house. Bob Graham used to talk about him as if Charlie came to the country before he did. Bob bought the ranch at Tatla Lake from Benny Franklin in 1902. He'd been in the country several years before that.

JAMES "SCOTTY" SHIELDS (1902–1991) *worked on the Cariboo Road for a year at the 141 Mile Ranch in return for a horse, before coming to the Chilcotin in 1924. He worked his way west to Eagle Lake country and went trapping at the south end of Chilko Lake. Along with others, Scotty was hired to shoot the herds of wild horses that roamed freely throughout the country, to make room for the introduction of cattle to the area. It was in this capacity that he had a run-in with Charlie Skinner, the man responsible for many of the wild horses in the first place.*

When I first got to know Charlie Skinner, he was working for the Chilco Ranch. He had been in to Eagle Lake then, before any cattle or anything was ever taken in there. He brought a bunch of horses up from the state of Washington. Nice horses, good horses. He took them in to Eagle Lake.

He built himself a little cabin at Kwatzine where the creek crosses the old road. The old road to Big Eagle Lake used to run on the north side of Kwatzine. He settled on Skinner Meadow and built a half-finished stopping house that still sits there today. It's a dove-tailed building, a real craftsman job. Frank Render built it. He was a top log builder. The CPR survey went through in 1867 and Old Skinner thought the railroad was going to go through there.

Now, how many horses he brought in, I don't know. There was an old story about how he was camped on the side of the road and had a nice team of horses hooked up on his wagon. And a chap came along and started talking to old Charlie, and he said: "That's a nice team of horses you're driving." And Charlie said: "Yep. And I got 40 more just like them." This chap he was talking to turned out to be the assessor. So he immediately jotted it down.

Old Skinner must have had over 400 head of horses but he couldn't round them up. Forestry told him he had to pay range fees on at least 40 head. He refused to do it, so they told him they were going to shoot them off.

The country was polluted with wild horses. The range was poorer

Louise's daughter Lucy Sulin, 1990.

than it is now. It was eaten right out because these horses were on it summer and winter. There was no livestock on it whatsoever. That is, nothing in the way of cattle or anything like that, just these horses.

Now the first bunch of horses Charley brought in were fairly gentle. They used to hang around his cabin at Kwatzine and you could walk up to some of them and pet them.

Now Charlie was given a good chance to sell as many of his horses as he could round up. He was offered the help from the Chilco Ranch to round up these good horses of his and they would have paid him so much a head. But he turned the offer down. He wouldn't sell them. You couldn't buy one from him let alone the bunch. He just wouldn't sell his horses. The result was he got old and couldn't do the riding like he used to and the horses ran and the studs weren't cut and they just bred and bred and bred until the whole country got polluted with horses.

You got to understand that everybody used horses to a great extent. They never counted them, they just kicked them loose on the range, and they joined the wild bunch too.

So Charlie Skinner came in to shoot me, so I was told. "I'm going to shoot that goddamn Scotty Shields because he's killing my horses."

Well I met him at his campfire right at his corral there at Eagle Lake, and he said nothing about killing me. I told him that I accidentally shot two of his old geldings that had his brand on, and that I didn't mean to. He took my word for it. Anyway he didn't kill me.

MACK SQUINAS *owns a small ranch down the Dean River from Anahim Lake. He remembers when Chiwid and Loozap were living around Anahim Lake.*

Chiwid's mother Loozap died up at Four Mile. I helped bring her body out. It was winter time. Deep snow.

We went up with a team and sleigh to pick her up. I forget where we buried her. Probably at the reserve. She was Ollie's mother, too.

I don't know what she was doing at Four Mile. She had a little cabin there. Chiwid was staying there too. Scotty Gregg was just a young boy.

JOSEPHINE GREGG *was born in the mountains of Kleena Kleene in the fall of 1925 while her parents, Lucy Sulin and Baptiste Dester were on a goat hunt. Her father was a half brother to Chiwid's husband Alec Jack, and Josephine married Chiwid's youngest half-brother Scotty Gregg.*

My first memory of Chiwid, we were camping at Charlotte Lake. I was four years old maybe. I barely remember. She was still living with Alec Jack then. I never saw her again for a long time.

Lillie was my husband, Scotty Gregg's oldest half-sister. My dad, Baptiste Dester was the half-brother of Lillie's husband, Alec Jack. Loozap was Scotty and Lillie's mother. She was from Redstone Band.

Loozap used to stay with Lillie. Camped all over the place.

BAPTISTE ELKINS *married Chiwid's half sister, Madeline Palmantier. His first wife was from Ulkatcho Village, and after her death, he and Madeline continued to live in Anahim Lake.*

First time I see Chiwid, at Eagle Lake when I was a kid. Across the river at Eagle Lake Henry's. Chiwid and his mother, he come around a little bit. They stay in a smokehouse.

Chiwid's mother don't talk. His name Loozap. He don't talk. He talk on his hand. He make a lot of kid, that old woman. Chiwid and Johnny Robertson, Scotty, and the youngest one I been married to. Loozap lived at Eagle Lake too . . .

We been looked after Loozap at Anahim Lake before he passed away. We can't do nothing. He can't eat and call nurse for him. Nurse can't do nothing for him too. He said: "I'm going to die anyway," he said. He can't do nothing for one week. Can't go toilet. No.

We bury him at Anahim Lake, Loozap. Some kind of Hunlin family.

FAULTS ON
BOTH SIDES

TOM CHIGNELL *preempted the Half Way Ranch near Tatla Lake, half way between Williams Lake and Bella Coola.*

When I first came out from England in 1920, the attitude toward the native people was very bad. They were frightfully poor and badly diseased. They were just getting over the flu of 1918 that killed at least half of them. Then the winter before I was here, they got the measles. And that killed them off just like flies. They couldn't fight it at all. They just laid down and died, you might say. It was very tough.

Most of the whites were good. They hired Indians ahead of whites if they could. They certainly preferred Indian riders and that kind of thing. Old Cotton, a Riske Creek rancher I worked for when I first came to the country, always had two or three Indian people there. He paid them properly, and they got the same food and everything that

FACING PAGE: *Eagle Lake Henry with "Mrs. Henry", Allietta.*

the whites who worked there got. Some people, of course, wouldn't have them at all. They wouldn't have an Indian around the place. I think there were faults on both sides.

IRENE BLISS *is still fond of the rustic way of life she experienced in the old days of the Chilcotin. Years ago her husband's parents had the first school in the country, at Willow Springs Ranch, where Irene lives today. Students from Tatla Lake, Redstone and Chezacut boarded at the Bliss residence so they could attend classes.*

Everybody, even the white people, used to live outside more when we were kids. We camped out a lot.

It was a three-week trip to go to Ashcroft with the freight wagons. Bill's dad used to make two trips a year. They'd go in May, and then again in the fall. You had to go when the grass was green for the horses.

Bill's father used to take the mail to Tatla Lake. He used to go to Alexis Creek and get it, and bring it back here in one day. The next day he'd go to Chilanko Forks, and the next day to Tatla Lake.

But this one time he wanted to be home for Christmas. He had to drive all the way from Tatla Lake back here in one night. He had a real fast team of Arabian mares, and he came by Redstone at midnight. They were all firing off their rifles at midnight on Christmas Eve.

He got back here at 3 o'clock in the morning. Fifty miles. That's a long way for a team. Especially pulling a sleigh . . .

My mother grew up with the Indians at Hanceville. And she had so many superstitions. There was always a scare. There was always a wildman somewhere. That was a big thing, a wildman.

One old woman with a little girl got up in the middle of the night. She was camped in the canyon and hitched up her team and drove up here. She was sitting on the veranda when we got up in the morning because there was a wildman around her camp.

And I remember over at Siwash Bridge, if you'd go over there. "Oh, a wildman here last night. He move my gun. I leave it right here, he move it over there." They really believed it, I think. They always did.

If an owl hooted just outside the house, they'd come in in the morning when they were haying or something. "I hear an owl last night. Somebody die, sure."

If there was a big wind, an important man . . . "A big Tyee die some place."

I can remember when we were haying at home one time when I was a teenager and we had this young Moise working for us. He used to sleep out in the hay pen. And he came in one morning just as white as a ghost. He looked just gastly. He said, "A coyote barked at me." That means he was going to die within the year. And I'll be darned if he didn't.

Things like that, that's what keeps the superstitions going, you know.

One time, not too many years ago, Lashaway Billy was going to build some fence for us over across the river. And he came down with his wagon and camped down by the spring. Bill and I were putting in the garden and we could hear this coyote barking down there. Just barking. Sometimes they howl and sometimes they bark. He was barking and running along the fence and we thought, "Good Heavens, Lashaway probably won't go over there. He'll be too scared. He'll think something's going to happen." But he went to work the next day anyway.

After a couple of days Bill went over to see how he was doing, and he said, "That coyote bark at me the other day, and he bring me good luck. One deer, he walk right in my camp and I shoot it."

My mother was as convinced as the Indians were. What ended the superstitions was the Indian kids being integrated in the schools.

BILL BLISS *led a colourful life in the frontier days of the Chilcotin. He knew many of the legendary characters, such as Eagle Lake Henry and Pete McCormick.*

My dad used to get groceries for the Bayliff Ranch, ours and the

Newtons. We used to take two wagons, one behind the other, and used a four-horse team. Sometimes a six-horse team.

The first time I went, I was seven years old, in 1916. Sometimes we'd bring back a mowing machine, a hay rake or a plough. We'd always have axes, horse shoes, nails. Everything you needed. There was a lot of freighting. In the early days there were no stores. You had to go to Ashcroft to get everything. Later there were stores at Alexis Creek, Hance's, Norman Lee's. They all had to have groceries hauled.

Sometimes they hauled grain in the winter on sleighs. They usually stayed at somebody's place who had hay, and always fed a little oats.

Pete McCormick was a great old packer. The first time I ever saw him he had an eight-horse team hauling two freight wagons from Ashcroft. He was stuck in the mud on this side of the Fraser River, on the Main Drag as they used to call it. Where you went down to the bridge below the Gang Ranch. Both wagons had heavy loads on them, and they were both in the mud deep. He uncoupled them and pulled one out, and then came back for the other . . .

I used to stay with Eagle Lake Henry. We shot horses together. There were hundreds and hundreds of horses shot in this country. Charlie Skinner's horses were all over the country. There were more than a thousand head shot.

Eagle Lake Henry was a nice guy 'til he got on the booze. Then look out. He took a drink whenever he could get it. Once in a while he made moonshine . . . peach whisky from fermented dried peaches. The kids cached all his guns and shells when they knew the stuff was going to come off the next day.

Henry had "white rights." He'd say: "I'm a whiteman just same as you." He was a good old guy alright. Not bad at all. He was a crack shot. If you were scared of him, he put on quite a show.

One night, he took the whisky off when I was there. Then he got out his gun and said he was going to shoot his old woman. She was sitting across the table and he had a six shooter and was pulling the trigger. I was pretty scared that any minute one was going to come that was alive. There were no shells in it, but I didn't know that. The kids must have hid the shells.

ILLA (HOLTE) GRAHAM *was three years old when she arrived in the Chilcotin with her family in 1923. Her family continued west to Tatla Lake, Kleena Kleene, Towdystan and Anahim Lake. Illa returned to Tatla Lake in 1944 to marry Alex Graham, and she helped run the ranch there for several years.*

Everybody, even the white people, used to camp around more. Only the game warden and the police had cars.

Life was simpler. People lived better than they do now. Not so pressured. That was the way of life, you didn't know any different. Indians and whites got along really good in them days. They didn't hardly fight.

Indians were well off, better than the white people. They had their own good horses, cattle, buckskin to sell, and beadwork. Now they got nothing.

Indians camped out and roughed it in the bush like the rest of us did. We wouldn't think anything of camping out in the winter, we all used to do it.

Nobody knew how Chiwid stood it. It was severely cold in them days. It would go down to 60 below zero. She just slowly went into the winter. After a long summer. Then just slowly her body got used to the cold. That's how she survived. It had to be. She didn't have a lot of blankets or sleeping bags or nothing.

In them days when I was a kid, people weren't anything like they are now. Things have gone backwards. Sulins, Cahooses, their word was as good as a bill of sale or written agreement. People used to stay at our house at Towdystan. We left the door unlocked and people stayed. We never had anything stolen. Now you leave your house open, you get robbed.

Old Sulin always used to say to my mom, "You got any meat?" And she'd say, "No." Then he'd say, "Okay. I'll get you meat." He'd be gone

Betty Graham at Tatla Lake, age 20. "Betty was the oldtime pioneer," remembers Laurie Haynes. "For twenty years she was the backbone of the Chilcotin."

a few hours and come back. He'd kill a moose and clean it and prop it open with sticks. Then my dad or mom or us kids would go get it.

PHIL ROBERTSON *was born in Alexis Creek in 1920, and grew up there. His father, Sandy Robertson, was a brother of Margaret Graham (Mrs. Bob Graham) of Tatla Lake. Phil's uncle, Jim Robertson, came to Canada from Scotland and settled in Nemiah Valley. He died there in 1916, four years before Phil was born. Chiwid's half-brother, Ollie Nukalow, is said to have been Jim's son. None of Sandy Robertson's children were ever told about Ollie Nukalow, who was also known as Johnny Robertson.*

Casimile Lulua told me I had a cousin in Anahim Lake. I went up there at stampede one time and he says: "You gonna see your cousin, eh?"

I said: "What cousin?"

"You got half-breed cousin. His name Robertson too. Must be cousin."

I told him he's full of you know what, and he laughed and he said: "You just high tone. You no want to talk to your cousin."

I just put it off and I never thought any more of it. I never did meet the guy. I thought he was kidding.

My brother-in-law, Al Elsey, knew Ollie Nukalow well. Said he was a pretty good fellow. Really good worker.

These oldtimers didn't want to tell their kids that the first ones in the country had Indian wives. The Indians know, but the whiteman don't want to admit it. When they get white families and white wives, they don't want to tell.

Same as those other oldtimers. When they first come here they had Indian ladies. Then when they get their imported brides from England, or wherever they come from, then they boot the Indian wife and kids out. There's lots of them in this country. Vivian Cahoose is Ollie's daughter.

One time one of Chiwid's daughters was in Tatla Lake Store with Tommy Lulua. She was trying to jawbone [get credit] from Betty Graham. This Indian girl had slightly red hair.

I guess Betty wasn't going to give any credit to her, so Tommy Lulua says to her: "What's the matter you, Betty. You don't give your sister jawbone?"

To Have a Witchdoctor Sing With Granny

CASIMILE LULUA *was born in the Eagle Lake country south of Tatla Lake and lived there all his life. For years he worked at the Graham Ranch in Tatla Lake and knew everyone who lived and worked in that part of the country.*

Chiwid and Alec Jack, together, and old Chiwid's mother, used to stay at Alec Jack Meadow on the way to Sucker Creek. North of Tatla Lake. They used to rustle cattle out for old Bob Graham. In those days, just go any place and cut some hay on crown land.

And it was around 40 below and Lester Dorsey, he come along.

Lester Dorsey, he was pretty young, and he went into Alec Jack's house. And he ask Alec Jack: "I can stay in your house for overnight?"

Alec said: "No fucking way."

FACING PAGE: *Tommy Holte, Alice (Engebretson) Holte, Illa Holte, Alex Graham, and Bill Graham at Tatla Lake, where the Holte children briefly attended school. Illa and Alex later married.*

And old Lester Dorsey beat the shit out of Alec Jack.

Still, he never stay overnight.

ALICE ENGEBRETSON *moved with her parents Andy and Ada Holte, and brother Tommy and sister Illa to the Engebretson ranch house at Towdystan in 1927. She knew Chiwid and Alec Jack very well over the five years her family lived at Towdystan.*

I was about 10 years old when I first met Chiwid. We lived at the Engebretson ranch house at Towdystan. Chiwid and Alec Jack were living at the Nimpo Meadow. They had two daughters, Cecilia and Julianna, who were a bit younger than us. But I remember them well.

Chiwid was a very sweet person. Nice looking and very kind. She was kind of tall, with a nice figure. She looked very good to me. She was good to all the children. She used to stay with my parents, while her husband Alec Jack was off chasing coyotes and wild horses with my dad . . .

Alec Jack was very violent. Especially with horses. Scotty [Gregg] said he was the meanest man he had ever seen. He said he especially didn't like anything that was female.

Scotty tells about him tying up a mare one time, and beating it with a logging chain. The horse retaliated and kicked him right in the stomach. Every time that horse saw Alec Jack, she took after him. Scotty said he sure thought that was a smart horse.

I saw some other tricks Alec Jack pulled. He was mean for no reason.

One time he and my dad ran some bear cubs up a tree. Then they got some sticks and poked the bears down and sicked the dogs on them. The bears were just screaming. I was 12 years old at the time, and went behind a tree to cry. I never got over that . . .

Alec Jack made homebrew, then the beatings would start.

It was March, when someone said Alec had killed her. The policeman Dan Weir came in, and dad took him over to Nimpo Lake

Meadow with his sleigh. When they brought Lillie out, she was nearly dead. She was bleeding awful bad, and they laid her out in the back of Dan Weir's police car. The car was a real mess.

Their daughters, Julianna and Cecilia, were at the Mission school in Williams Lake. The authorities told Chiwid never to go back to Alec Jack again. Then he retaliated, and wouldn't let the girls see their mother.

My parents never told me Chiwid was beat up or sewed up or anything. It was a sign of the times. I was 16 years old, and they hid everything.

Alec Jack had his good points and was a great friend of the white people. He was a good worker and built a nice house and barn. He put up good hay and good corrals. His half brother, Baptiste Dester, could not speak as good English as he could . . .

I remember when Alec Jack left the country. He had some cows and a few horses, and was having trouble with a blue mare that ran away. Tommy Holte, my brother, said to him, "If you'd been good to your wife you'd have her to help you now."

Lillie lived around Anahim Lake on her own for about twenty years after she and Alec split up. Then she had a third daughter, Mary Jane. The baby was born at the old Lester Dorsey place. In a tent, under a spruce tree. It was the year after Dave Dorsey was born. Jane Leeman attended the birth, and all the men were teasing about whose baby it was.

Mrs. Bryant gave the baby milk and everything, and a few years later Jane eventually took the child away from Chiwid because there were reports that she was starving it. She kept the baby for two months because it had malnutrition. That little girl was just skin and bones, but she was very good natured. She wouldn't cry about anything. The little girl stayed outside with Chiwid. When she was old enough to go to school, they sent her off to St. Joseph's Mission, near Williams Lake. She was adopted by a family from Anaham Reserve near Alexis Creek.

ILLA GRAHAM *was seven years old when her family moved to the Engebretson ranch house at Towdystan.*

She was bright when I first knew her, but her husband used to beat her up so much she got mental. Alec Jack was always beating her up. They'd get to drinking or whatever, and he'd get into a tantrum over a cow dying or something, and would go on a rampage.

Dad used to go down and see if he could stop Alec from beating her up so bad. Ollie Nukalow, Chiwid's half-brother, was only a kid of 14 or 15 at the time. He'd ride over and get my dad. Then dad would have to ride over to Nimpo Lake to quiet old Alec down. He'd cross by the fish trap and go in that way.

WILF HODGSON *drove the freight truck into the Chilcotin from Williams Lake after taking over the business from his father Tommy, who founded Hodgson's Freightlines in 1910.*

My dad told me one time he was pretty handy. Old Alec had an old car with wooden spokes. I guess the old spokes were broken and he was stuck on the road, when my dad went by with the freight truck.

By the time my dad had come back, by God, Alec had made new spokes for the old car and fit them in there, and away he went.

HANK LAW *lived in the Chilcotin on two different occasions. In 1931 he arrived on his bicycle from Vancouver. When he got to Riske Creek he traded his bike for a saddle horse. "Not many Indians had seen a bicycle in those days." He got married in Tatlayoko, then left the country to serve in World War II. In 1960 he returned to Puntzi to work at the air base. He then bought the old Pyper place at Pyper Lake.*

I first met Chiwid the year she got in that mixup with her man. He beat her up with a logging chain and cut her with a knife.

I was building an annex on the Red Cross outpost hospital at Alexis Creek in 1932–33 when Dr. Knipthal called me into the hospital to show off his stitching job of sewing her back up. He was taking off the bandages and she was sitting on a high stool.

She looked young, maybe 18 or 20 years old, and the doctor was very proud of his work.

I saw her on and off, pretty near every year after that. She used to travel with a couple of pack horses and a saddle horse from Chezacut way. She went from Tatla Lake on out to Stone. She never went in a house, and that always upset the do-gooders. They always said, "She can't do this," and "She can't do that." But she outlived most of these can't-doers.

Eventually she got rid of her horses, and travelled by foot. She'd shoot a moose with a bent up old .22, and camp right there until she and the bears and the coyotes had eaten it all up.

I got married in Tatlayoko in 1935, and didn't see Chiwid again until we moved back to Alexis Creek in 1937. Then I went to war for five years, and didn't move back to the Chilcotin until 1960. We went to Puntzi, and I worked at the air force base there. Then we got the old Pyper place at Pyper Lake. That's where I saw Chiwid again.

She had got rid of her horses by the time I moved to Pyper Lake. When she wanted to move camp, she had quite a way of doing it. She had all her stuff tied in several bundles. When she moved these bundles, she did it so she could always keep an eye on them. I guess Indian kids used to steal stuff from her. She threatened to shoot them with her .22 if they didn't quit.

Lillie Skinner got her name from the chickadee. It's said that Chiwid is the Indian name for chickadee.

The name comes from the sound the bird makes. In January, it goes "chee-wit." In February, "chee-chee-wit," and in March it goes "chee-chee-chee-wit."

Chiwid used to be on my place at Pyper Lake when the suckers were running in the spring. When you saw the eagles sitting in the trees above the creek, you knew Chiwid was there. She'd be camped along the creek, catching the suckers in her net.

She spent several winters at Pyper Lake while we were there. It could be 60 below out there. And the bloody lake would be cracking.

And the timbers cracking. And the northern lights shimmering in your face. And she'd be quite comfortable. Well I don't know how comfortable, but she'd be breathing the next morning. And that's what it's all about. It's surprising what you can stand if you have to . . .

She'd talk to me, or to anybody else she knew. Just the odd word. But any man she had never seen, she'd just ignore them. Just turn around and walk the other way. She took to me okay. She was quite normal. But she was still quite aloof. She had this thing in her mind to live away from other people.

One time at Pyper Lake, this young fellow and I had some cows we wanted to find. We took off from my place early in the morning, and were going by the swimming hole, when my friend said he could smell smoke. Well, it was fall time . . . hunting time, and since it was my range, I decided to take a look around. Then I saw a wisp of smoke, and saw what looked like a bedroll right up close to the fire.

So I barrelled down there, and this other fellow with me. We had a dog with us. As soon as I got close, I could see who it was. It was Chiwid. She had a bunch of rags over her and a few old cans and a frying pan, and that was it.

So I'm standing there. I got off my horse, and had the horse on one side and the dog on the other. She reared up and threw the clothes off her, and spit out a big gob of tobacco juice. Then she stood up and talked to me. We were standing there talking, and all of a sudden she froze. Just froze, and she's listening. And you know it must have been two minutes later that my horse looked, and my dog looked. Two minutes after she could hear whatever it was moving in the bush.

That's how she was. She was way ahead of the animals to hear anything or smell anything.

One time she was heading up to my place, and I was coming up the trail behind her on a saddle horse. She kind of stopped when she heard me coming, and waited for me to go by. When she saw it was me, she stopped and said: "Howdy."

I asked her what the problem was, and she said: "I smell'em

skunk." Then she pointed up the hill. That's where I was going, so I left her there and took off. You know, two days later there was a skunk in there. But she bloody well knew way before it happened. This is how she was.

I've seen her take her moccasin rubber off, and have no moccasins on. Just bare feet. And empty the snow out. You know how cold it is when you can empty the snow out, and it's just like sugar? Anybody else would freeze, but not the old lady. She wasn't all bundled up in clothes. She had no sleeping bag. It was just a pile of old clothes and rags.

I was giving her a ride one time from the store to her camp at Pyper Lake. I picked up this bag of stuff to take to her camp, and felt the bag bust. So I quickly put it down before anything could spill out. It was the sugar sack that had busted, and some of the sugar spilled on the ground.

You know, she went and got an old can, and was on her hands and knees. I think she picked up every grain of sugar there was. She wasn't going to waste it, that's for sure.

LOUISA JEFF *used to play with Loozap's youngest daughter Madeline when they were young children. She lived most of her life in the Riske Creek area.*

Alec Jack used to come on a horse and stay a few days at my house at Riske Creek. Then he would keep going on to Toosey. He was a really easy-going guy. He don't rush about anything. A really calm person, he takes his time.

One time, Edith Inscho used to stay with Alec Jack, and she said he was mean. He used to get mad at people wherever he stayed. Then he'd just pack his stuff and leave.

Alec Jack used to always beat Chiwid up. One time he beat her up so bad that she almost died. After that she spent most of her time living in a tent outdoors. No tent, just a little fire. Sit beside the fire, that's all. She didn't like living in a house. She always liked to be outside beside a campfire.

PHIL ROBERTSON *was born in Alexis Creek and grew up in the Chilcotin.*

I was a little kid going to school in Alexis Creek when the policeman, Bill Broughton, arrested Alec Jack. The jailhouse was his office, and he'd turn him in there and got a cot for him.

Alec didn't want to leave. He was eating real good and had a roof over his head. His punishment was splitting wood during the day. Bill Broughton had Alec splitting a whole bunch of wood for the police station. Then at night, they'd lock him up in the office.

We used to go down there and talk to him. We didn't know he was a bad guy. So, after a while, Mrs. Broughton gave us a talking-to. She said: "You stay away from that guy." So we had to stay away.

Mrs. Broughton told us he had beat Lillie up. He hit her with a harness butt-chain. It kind of crippled her up.

RANDOLPH MULVAHILL *was born in 1917 at Chezacut Lake. He ranched in Chezacut all his life before retiring to Alexis Creek in the late 1980s. "I was raised with the Indian and I know him inside out. Sometimes I can read him six months ahead of what he's going to do." Randolph owned the last of the great Chilcotin horse herds. "One time, I had over 500 head of horses. I left them out, never run them on the ranch. That's how come they got so wild. I sold more horses than any one man in North America over a couple of years during the sixties."*

Alec Jack came down here, and we looked after his horses for him when they took Chiwid to Vancouver after she got that beating up that made her haywire. He sold all his cattle to my dad and spent money on her trying to bring her out of it. But it never really straightened up.

But God damn, she was a beautiful woman then. Hard to believe. She's straight half-breed . . . Charlie Skinner's daughter. Damn, she was a good looking woman. One of those people who didn't have to do anything. She's just good looking. She could have been all mud and dirt out of the gutter, and she was still good looking. You see the odd person like that, and she was one of them.

I guess she was a hell of a good woman 'til he knocked her head haywire with a logging chain. That's what George Granbush told me. It was a double logging chain around her head.

She was hurt bad enough that Alec brought her out from Anahim Lake to Chezacut. He knew my dad good, and sold him his cattle. The old man give him a bunch of money, then took him and her to Williams Lake. Then they took her to Vancouver, and he went down with her. It was around 1928, and the old man wintered their horses for them. There was a mare and a colt, a pack horse, her saddle horse and his. We fed them right there, all winter. I remember it well.

In the spring they came back and they got their horses and went back to Anahim Lake.

ROSALIE DAWN HAINES *is the daughter of Julianna Setah and the granddaughter of Chiwid. She lives in the Tsilhqot'in community of Stone.*

Grandfather Alec used to have a horse named Peanuts and he used to ride over from Stone every spring to see us at Big Creek. He would always bring us kids a couple bags of peanuts.

He sold his cattle off to have a witchdoctor sing with Granny.

HARRY HAYNES *ranched for years in Tatlayoko Valley after arriving in the country in 1929. He knew Alec Jack and Chiwid well, but never knew them as a couple.*

Lou fed cattle for Sandy Robertson in Nemiah Valley one year. He got short of grub, so he had to go out. So he went to Hanceville, and they'd run a big batch of booze off their still. When he got there everybody was partying to beat hell. In fact there was some already laid out. And he had a few drinks himself, and he got sick. But he only had a few drinks. He got sick, so he quit drinking.

Julianna Setah at Stone, 1988.

So, next morning when he went to go get his sled and get loaded up and head for home, everybody was sick. They were throwing up all over the place. I guess they didn't get rid of all the fusel oil out of it, and everybody was sick. Anyhow, he was at the store loading up, and old Percy Hance came out and said: "Lou, you going to go past Grover's cabin?"

And Lou said: "Yeah, I'm going to probably stay with him tonight."

Well Percy comes out with a gallon jug of this stuff and he said: "Well, give this to Grover. He'll enjoy it."

So Lou finally got up to Grover's place and pulled in front of the cabin with the sled, and Grover opened the door and hollered at him: "Hey Lou, how you doing!"

Lou reached down and brings this jug up. He said: "Percy sent you a present."

Grover grabbed that jug and he run in the house and he said: "You put your horses away and I'll cook supper."

Well, Lou put the horses away and fed them and everything and come in the house. Grover never thought about cooking any supper. He had about two inches out of that jug already. Before the evening was over a mouse ran across the floor. Grover grabbed his 30-30 and he shot that mouse. Then, after that, he started shooting the knotholes in the cabin.

Well, Grover eventually passed out. I guess he was so drunk he passed out and got sick laying flat on his back. He threw up all over the bed and all over himself, and oh God, Lou said it was an awful mess. He said he was glad to get out of there.

Anyhow, Lou got his horses all hooked up and everything all ready to go, and he just stepped in the cabin to say good-bye. Grover was sitting on the edge of the bed. "What a stink," he said.

And Lou said, "I'm going, Grover. I got to get going. I got to feed cattle yet today, when I get home."

And Grover says, "Okay, Lou."

So, Lou went out of the house and climbed in his sled, and Grover opens the door and says: "Are you going past Alec Jack's cabin, Lou?"

And Lou says, "Yeah, I'm going right past the cabin."

So, he had this jug behind the door and he brings it out and says, "Here Lou. Give this to Alec Jack. I never did like the son of a bitch."

JULIANNA SETAH, *born in 1922, is Chiwid's second oldest daughter. She says Bob Graham was her and her sister Cecilia's real father. But they were both raised as Alec Jack's children. At an early age, Julianna and Cecilia were sent to the St. Joseph's Mission residential school near Williams Lake. It was while they were there that Chiwid suffered the terrible beating from Alec Jack that changed her life. From then on, the two girls were cared for by the Henry Dick family at the Tsilhqot'in village of Anaham. Julianna married Willie George Setah and they spent several years in the Eagle Lake country until their oldest children were ready for school. Then they moved to Big Creek for 30 years.*

We just drifted around from place to place. That's how we were raised. Henry Dick from Anaham Reserve used to take us in, when we got out of the Mission [St. Joseph's]. Dad used to buy him some groceries for us.

As children, we used to cry a lot. We were lonely and didn't like it when our mom would stay outside all the time. Sometimes she would move away and not tell us.

After He
Went Crazy

MARY ANN ROSS *was born at Kleena Kleene in 1913 and grew up on a trapline in the rugged Kleena Kleene country. Her grandfather, Chief One Eye Charlie, was discovered shot in the back shortly before Mary Ann was born. His murderer was never found out.*

I seen Chiwid lots of times. We lived in the same country. But he lived out in the bush where he find grass to cut hay for his horse. Doug Boyd told me that at Eagle Lake, Lillie sleep right on the cattle trail, where the cattle come out on the flat. She was sleeping right there. Got no tent, nothing. Just sleep and cover himself up. That's the way he camp.

And a whole bunch of cattle coming out, he said. Doug was driving these cattle. And Chiwid jump up there and he's shaking his blanket. And he scare up all the cattle.

FACING PAGE: *Francis William, Eddie William, Euphrasia William with Mabel William's little girl, Mabel William holding her infant daughter, and Eugene William.*

That's how he sleep. A lot of bear out in that country, too. Just sleep with his .22. Bed down any place. He shot a moose with a .22. When he need some meat, he get him . . .

Chiwid's mother couldn't talk. Just a single mother. He born and raised close to the mountain country of Tatla Lake, Redstone, Nemiah Valley. Then stay at Nimpo Lake. Then his mother went blind. Nobody look after him much.

Chiwid married Alec Jack. They had two daughter. Kids grow up and they go. After that they fight each other too much, and they left one another. Alec Jack he go his way, and old Lillie he go any place to live. Just travel around. Find a meadow, cut the hay. He had a scythe and a butcher knife. He had one horse and seven cow that time.

Pretty tough woman, Chiwid. Just come somewhere and make a little fire. That's all. He don't bother to put up his tent. Just sit there like a little muskrat.

Then he travel. He travel around lots. He go another place. He stay for the winter. Sometime he go all the way to Anahim Lake to stay for the winter. I guess he make fire under a spruce tree. And that's his home.

I talk with him lots. There's nothing wrong with him. That's just his way of life, I guess. Nobody try to help him.

Chiwid looked like his daughter when he was young. Same tall. Kind of tall and slim. But one foot went lame. I guess when he was young his foot kind of out of place. No doctor to fix it. Kind of hard to walk on that one. But he do all that work with it. Kind of lumped on one side a little bit. But he sure worked. Made his own living.

No welfare them days. Just got to go out. Always make out somehow. Always get the fish or meat or something. Well, he sell the cow once in a while. Got the flour, sugar, tea. He have them. Rice or something.

He don't carry much when he go some place. Put a little in his pocket. Don't have no big bunch of dishes or nothing. You find his camp, it looks like nobody stay. Maybe one little can. He used to use a can to make tea. Just one cup of tea. So you don't carry too many pots.

EUPHRASIA WILLIAM was raised in the Redbrush area north of Redstone. Her family's traditional territory stretched from Redbrush to the Kleena Kleene mountains. Euphrasia and her family moved with the seasons, camping from spring until freeze-up in the fall.

When I was 10 years old, we moved to Redbrush. My brother, my daddy and me.

One winter, the snow was pretty deep. We were going to sell our fur at the store, about three miles away. We got up early, the three of us. And we started to walk across. Outside on the snow, Lillie Skinner sleeping on her blanket. Just like an animal, that Lillie Skinner. And we were passing her, and we told her: "We're going to sell our squirrel over there." And she got up on her blanket, and the snow fell off. We pass her and go to meet the sleigh on the other side.

We sell our squirrel. Just five cents that's all. We're poor that time. We sell that squirrel and give the money to our daddy for a little sugar. That's what we are doing before. We're all poor, you know. That time we couldn't even change our clothes. That's a long time ago, I'm telling you. Now I'm not like that. Now I got everything . . .

Lillie, she just live any place beside the fire. Anahim Lake, Towdystan. Just a small fire. Just burn little sticks. When she stay with you. It's kind of cold and she still live outside. Just like an animal, I guess. Everytime she comes inside the house she can't get warm. "Cold, ooh cold!" she said. And she go outside. She's not cold outside. Just like an animal.

She was singing one time. She thinking just like a coyote.

Maybe her body's just like something. Some kind of old animal. That's why she do that. She just think of something. Must be like that. She thinks she's a coyote. That's how she stays warm.

DONALD EKKS continues to move about the country with the seasonss much the way Chiwid did. He and his wife Emily have several camps. There is one important difference: Donald's camps are well equipped with warm log cabins, good stoves and heaters and plenty of firewood.

When I first got to know Chiwid, she had a little a girl. A papoose, just a little one. She stayed at Anahim Lake all the time. Before that, Chiwid stayed with her husband Alec Jack, near Nimpo Lake. They had a house on a mountain meadow, seven miles west of Nimpo Lake. Gus Cahoose's meadow. Sure nice country. Nice meadow. House way up on a hill. Lake with some kind of fish. Nice spring water. That's the place Chiwid had a cabin.

Then one day she got sick. She came all the way back to Anahim Lake. Never went back. Alec Jack and Chiwid both got sick. Too much lonesome, I guess. Nobody around.

After that, she quit that man. Chiwid came back and stayed quite a while at Towdystan. Then she stayed around Tatla Lake and Redstone. Maybe just stay one place one year. Just travel around. Can't stay just one place. Always moving . . .

She came this way, riding saddle horse to Potato Mountain. The next day she was over there in Tatlayoko. We saw Chiwid all over. One time fishing at Kwatzine Lake, another time at Clearwater.

One time Alex Graham saw two canoes, one behind the other, going across Tatla Lake. Alex didn't know who it was. Then he figured it was Chiwid packing her stuff across the lake . . .

Chiwid told stories, too. Lots of oldtimer stories. She'd talk about going down to Bella Coola with her pack horse and her mom. She used to travel around quite a bit with her husband, Alec Jack, as well.

I guess they went down to Stuie and the stampede, a long time ago. Chiwid's mother stay in Bella Coola quite a bit. For two or three winters. She had a good friend there. A Bella Coola Indian. I guess Chiwid went along, but she never like to stay in Bella Coola too long.

"Not much good, Bella Coola," Chiwid say.

When she visit you, she camp pretty far away. She was scared of people. Maybe she was scared somebody would steal her stuff. But she didn't have much good stuff. Just old junk she got from the dump.

David, my boy, laugh like hell. I guess he saw her some place, and tried and look in her sack. Chiwid get mad.

"Don't try and steal it," she said.

My dad, Charlie Ekks, he didn't like Chiwid. No. Chiwid, she don't like my dad either.

"Old Ekks . . . no good for nothing," she'd say.

I guess my dad made jokes on her. Ekks make'em lot of fun with Chiwid. No, she don't like my dad.

I'd see Chiwid mostly in the summer. Nobody see her much in winter. She just camped in the bush. Just lay down, and slept anywhere. Just like a coyote or a dog. In the winter she just put a few little jackpine branches under her, and make little fire. No tent. Just cover up with a blanket. Sometimes she take a few little sticks, and make a kind of lean-to. Like a house. She stay right under. But it wasn't very warm. When it rain or snow, she just cover up her stuff. I guess she get wet lots of times. Sure funny woman.

In her camp, all she have was frying pan. Lots of kettle, and lots of grub. A long time ago she got an old age pension. She got all kinds of grub. Lots of sugar and potatoes.

One time, Chiwid stay at Kwatzine Lake when Henry Lulua was there. He saw her walk right up to her waist to get water. She went for a swim every morning at 4:30 or 5. Pretty cold. When Henry first saw her, he thought she was a bear.

Pretty tough woman.

THOMAS SQUINAS (1906–1994) *was born at Anahim Lake. His father, Chief Domas Squinas, had the only residence in the Anahim Lake area until the 1920s when an influx of settlers arrived to "take up land." Domas established one of the first ranches in the area, which Thomas inherited. He first met Chiwid when she was living with Alec Jack at Nimpo Lake Meadow. Many say Thomas was the father of Chiwid's third child, Mary Jane.*

I know Chiwid. Lots of times I used to tease him. He was my girlfriend one time. He was a nice looking girl when he was young. But his husband Alec Jack kick him in the head or something. That's why he go crazy a little bit. When he got old, he got dirty. After he went crazy.

Sometimes, Chiwid lived inside, but I don't know. He used to say: "Camp out better."

People tell him: "You're going to freeze to death. Better come inside."

"Oh," he say. "I don't like it inside a house. Want to stay out. Stay with wild animals," he say. "That's what I like . . . cold. Best is cold place."

One time, I go way down Tatla Lake country. He got a campfire there. Snow in a kettle to melt it for water.

How he stay outside all the time, I don't know. That's what I wonder. I don't know how he can stand that . . . 40 below, you know? Camp out. Just smoke . . . too cold . . . not even a hot fire. Lots of wood there, but too cold. You know, 40 below and just a smoke come out . . .

When lots of people come, he's just like a wild animal after a while. Too much in his head, I guess. Sees a whiteman coming, he climb a tree. I hear about it, but I never see him do that.

One time, my wife and I took a trip some place. Maybe down to Burns Lake. We took saddle horses. Maybe gone two weeks. Chiwid was camped at Corkscrew Creek, right by our ranch. And we leave him here. Tell him we are going, and don't want to leave the place without somebody to watch it. We had 300 head of sheep, about 100 head of cows, and lots of horses.

My wife said: "Chiwid, you stay here." He gave him a job. "You watch, and camp over there someplace."

So then, we took off. When we got back, about two weeks later, Chiwid got a smoke house. Cook that sheep. Got a campfire and smoke the sheep beside the fire on a stick. He killed some. Too many, though. Maybe three, four or five. Cook it and eat it too, and smoke some too.

Yeah, must be he can't help it, do that. Used to be he don't do that. He was a nice lady. Nice looking lady, too.

JOSEPHINE GREGG *knew Chiwid and Alec Jack all her life. Her father, Baptiste Dester, was Alec's half-brother. In 1948, Josephine married Chiwid's half-brother, Scotty Gregg, and they lived together at Clearwater Lake.*

That first summer after Lillie and Alec Jack split up, Lillie worked for Eagle Lake Henry at Mountain House near Chilko Lake, across the Chilko River. That's how he got his saddle horse and saddle. Then he moved back to Anahim Lake and lived on his own. He stayed around Morrison Meadow, Fish Trap and Cless Pocket. A year later his little girl, Mary Jane, was born.

Most of the time, Lillie stayed with the Sulin family at Fish Trap. He stayed with us too, at Cless Pocket. He didn't stay outside. He had a little cabin or a tent.

After Mary Jane wasn't with him any more, then Lillie never bother to set up his tent. He just stayed anywhere, in an open place. He kept doing that. Moving around. Living all over the country. Oldtimers used to live like that too. All over the country. Living by themselves.

Lillie took care of Mary Jane until he was old enough to go to school. He was too mean to that little girl. Father Hennessy was the teacher at Redbrush. He saw her chase that girl around with a pitchfork, and told the cops or somebody. Then they take the kid away.

LOUISA JEFF *was raised in the Riske Creek area. As part of their seasonal round, her family used to travel 150 kilometres by saddle horse to Tatlayoko to dig wild potatoes. Chiwid travelled even further, from Anahim Lake to Riske Creek, with her young daughter Mary Jane, often walking much of the way.*

My real mom traded me for a sack of flour when I was a baby. The people that raised me, their last name was Billy.

When I was a little girl, I played with Chiwid's sister, Madeline. Their mother's name was Loozap. She was deaf and dumb. Not much talk, I think.

A long time ago, lots of people from all over the Chilcotin used to come down to Toosey in their wagons to pick berries. There's lots of dik [saskatoon berries] and chokecherries down there.

When I was a little girl, we used to ride a saddle horse all the way to Tatlayoko to pick wild potatoes. There were lots of dik there too. Lots of hooshum berries in Tatlayoko. I make lots of hooshum berries.

A long time ago, Chiwid used to stay around Tatlayoko and Kleena Kleene. A long time ago she was strong and used to pull a little pack horse. Her daughter used to walk behind with bare feet. One time, they came to Toosey to pick berries. A long time ago she do that. She and her daughter.

They took Mary Jane away from Chiwid because she was living too poor with her. She was always walking around barefoot, behind the pack horse. They didn't like to see her walking with bare feet all the time, living that way with Chiwid.

LEE BUTLER *was born in the Red Cross Outpost Clinic in Alexis Creek in 1931. His father, Leonard Butler, arrived in the Chilcotin from the United States in the 1920s and settled in the West Branch Valley where he married Hilda McKill. Hilda's mother was part Tsilhqot'in and born at Soda Creek. Lee has lived all his life at Bluff Lake in the West Branch Valley where he ranches and drives the school bus.*

I'd see Chiwid once or twice every summer, camped along the swamp somewhere along the old West Branch Road. One of her main camping areas was along the Hook Lake shortcut trail to Tatla Lake.

When I was a little kid, I remember seeing her camped with her daughters at a little pothole meadow, not too far from the Little Sapeye Lake turnoff. The girls were pretty grown up by then. We call it Rush Lake. There used to be water in there and the Indians used to camp there every spring and come down to Little Sapeye Creek to catch fish.

One spring, Jim Brown, a prospector from Kleena Kleene, came along. He decided he was going to camp with them all night. But they didn't think he should do that.

He started to set up camp right beside them, but they chased him out of there and shot his pack horse. Killed it right there. I was about 12 or 13 years old at the time, and remember that horse laying there all summer.

That scared old Jim pretty bad. He came down to our place and got ahold of dad and tried to get dad to call the police. Dad wouldn't do it. He told Jim he shouldn't have been there in the first place. He loaned him a pack horse to get all his stuff out of there.

Chiwid was a great shot. She lived with her old single-shot .22 Cooey. That was one thing I always noticed when I rode past her camp. She always had that gun leaning up against a tree.

She probably used that .22 to shoot Jim's horse.

SUSAN CAHOOSE, *born in 1930, is the daughter of Sam and Mary Sulin of Fish Trap near Nimpo Lake. Susan has lived all her life where the Dean River flows out of Nimpo Lake. Her mother and Chiwid were good friends and she remembers Chiwid from early childhood.*

She stayed one year at our place, camped on the other side of the hill by Teddy's house. She stayed one winter, and made hay for her horse in the meadow right behind. That time she didn't have any cows. She cut hay with a scythe, and cut a blanket in half to pack the hay in two big bundles on either side of her horse.

She don't trust anybody. She hauled all her hay to her camp. It sure took a long time for her to haul that hay all the way across from the meadow.

She was sure smart, that Chiwid. She make a lean-to out of small trees and make a fire right in the middle. Small tree like this, pile up, pile up, pile up.

When we were lonesome, my sister and I would go down there and talk to her. Me and my oldest sister, Amelia.

At Christmas time, my dad, Sam Sulin, make homebrew. My mom tell me and my sister: "Go get Chiwid. Christmas time. Have party with us." So we go get her. Tell her: "Mom want to see you." So we bring Chiwid down. One night or one day, she stay with us. I don't remember. Yeah, she stayed one year over there.

One time, she camped over by the holding grounds, down the Morrison Meadow road. She stayed one year there too.

On this side of the jackpine, there's lots of timber. But she don't care. She camped over there. That time she had some cows. About six, or something like that. Her brother, that one who died logging in Bella Coola, Ollie, he worried about his sister. He went down there and brought her a tent. But she just packed it around. She don't use it. The tent stayed folded up the whole time. She just use a little bit of plastic and a lean-to.

Ollie went down there to help her with her cows. To make them stay in one bunch. He set that tent up for her, and stayed with her too. That time she wasn't very strong. He made wood for her and every-thing. And watched her cows.

Then at Christmas, my mom told me again: "Go down and get Chiwid." Chiwid and my mom stayed together all the time. They were good friends a long time before I was born. Chiwid and my mom would go hunt squirrels together.

I don't know where Mary Jane was born, but I knew her when she was still in a basket at Morrison Meadow. I was about seven years old. We saw Chiwid coming. Me and my sister we liked that kid. Packed her around and everything.

She had one small colt, and Chiwid made him into a pack horse. She rode her horse and that kid would come along behind. Chiwid, her mind not good. Every place she'd go, that kid would walk behind that little colt pack horse. Start moving. That little girl just walked behind. That little colt pack horse was too young. The pack was too heavy, and his back go like this. Get humped up right in the middle of his back. Pretty soon he died down at the holding grounds.

Her mind not too good, Chiwid.

She lost another horse at Chilanko one time. The horse cut in its belly. It was packing an axe when it started to buck. The axe cut the horse. That's how she lose that horse down at Chilanko.

Chiwid used to put money in a can and bury it. Lots of money. She don't use it. It's still there yet, in that big swamp by Chilanko.

Chiwid stayed by a small fire all day in the winter. I used to get cold when I went to visit her. She would say: "As soon as you get cold . . . you put little bit of fire . . . you warm up . . . you warm up." As soon as the fire goes out, she'd put another little bit of wood in there.

Sure tough, that woman. That's what I remember about Chiwid. There's not many people in this country like her any more. I don't think so.

Once TOM CHIGNELL *established the Half Way Ranch a few miles west of Tatla Lake, he got a job working for the Dominion Telegraph Company as a lineman. For many years he kept the line between Chilanko Forks and the Bella Coola Hill clear of fallen trees and other problems. Because he was on the road so much, he designed a camper for the back of his 1-ton flat-deck truck.*

I first met Chiwid around 1930. She and I were always good friends. I never gave her any reason not to be a friend of mine. She was badly abused by her own people, and also by some of the whites as well.

Once she came hobbling out over the trail from Smokey Lake, and came down to my place. She was in an awful mess. Two Indians who were going back from the Anahim Stampede had grabbed her and raped her. Then they simply beat her up and turned her loose. She had to walk about seven miles from where this happened down to my place.

Chiwid and Alec Jack were separated by the time I got to know them. I never knew them as a couple. She was always alone. Just traveling up and down the road, carrying four or five or more sacks of clothes and that sort of thing. She'd take them on ahead half a mile, then come on back and get the next one. She'd cache it off in the woods, and spend all day just moving camp like that. A lot of people, like the freight truck drivers and people like that, would always look for her along the road. They'd always pick her up and put her off wherever she wanted to get off. Some place right out in the sticks, where she knew she left a cache of clothes and that sort of thing.

She'd get rides with Hodgsons or any of these people driving the road. I think I was one of her favorites because I was up and down the road so much in those days, working on the telegraph line.

People thought she was a little crazy, but she certainly did nobody any harm. If Chiwid ever got the idea you were "laying for her" she'd give you a very wide berth. But she used to "lay for me" when she wanted to move camp.

I used to stop for her, and would load four, five or six gunny sacks on the back of the truck. Put her in the cab and go up the road. Then "Stop, stop, stop!" And then she'd get out and I'd take her sacks and pack them fifteen or twenty yards off into the woods where she wanted them. Then away she'd go. And I'd go on about my business too . . .

One winter after Eve and I were married, Chiwid came into our old house. She had a horse at that time. She came in quite late one Sunday night, and I heard something outside. I suppose the dog barked or something of that kind, and I went out and here was the poor old soul outside there.

I put an arm around her and took her into the house. I forget what the temperature was. It was between 40 and 50 below zero. I turned her over to Eve, and she got her into a chair and gave her some warm soup. I went out and got her horse.

The next day on my way to Kleena Kleene, I could see three places between the house and the end of the flat, in a half a mile stretch, where she and the horse had laid down on the side of the road. The horse and her at the same time. Both of them were just all in, that was all. She stayed with us that time, two or three nights. And got warmed up, and fed up too. And I fed the horse of course.

It was unusual for her to come in at all. But I think she was just desperate, that was all there was to it. It was just touch and go whether she was even going to make it.

She used to bring me fish. Great big long fish. She couldn't even carry them without their tails dragging. Where she ever got them, I never could understand. If they came out of One Eye Lake, that was a long way to carry them. About seven miles. She'd bring these damn things, and they'd weigh anywhere from five to ten pounds. But she'd bring them in. She'd take something for them. A little tea or sugar, or anything like that. She really appreciated those sort of things, so I used to think it was a really good trade for her. I used to eat the fish sometimes too. I don't think my wife ever did as far as that goes, because they were very often just a little bit on the stale side. But I would eat them.

She didn't speak very good English, but she could make herself understood. She didn't actually speak very much. Mostly just signs. You were supposed to know what she wanted. I always did know. I knew that she wanted a ride some place and to take her camp. As soon as she had the place all picked out, she'd nudge my arm and point down there, and we'd stop. Of course there wasn't very much traffic in those days. In fact there was very, very little.

Chiwid was unusual from other Indian people, going off alone and being by herself so much. I don't think the Chilcotin people traditionally lived in absolute solitude like she did for so much of the time. She was absolutely alone, and I think she preferred it that way too.

Thomas Squinas at Nimpo Lake, 1987.

DORIS LULUA *knew Chiwid and Alec Jack from her earliest childhood. She has lived her whole life in the Eagle Lake country south of Tatla Lake.*

Lilllie just go by himself. She don't need nobody. When she's going to camp, always go a long ways from other people before she's going to set up camp.

Every summer she go up the mountain. And just she had one horse. I don't know how the hell can she move. And she go up the mountain and she can't kill no deer. And just live on straight potatoes. And she got just tea and sugar is about all she got.

She told my mom, "Pretty soon I starve to death, I'm really hungry." And my mom she give him meat. And she don't got no tent. Just underneath that mountain tree. She got a couple blanket and one for that little girl, Henry's wife. She go with him. Put the pack on the horse and that little girl she comin' behind that horse. And she walk all the way down Potato Mountain. Steep hill too.

She dig lots of potatoes. She pack 'em down. Just pack on one horse. She bring down to the bottom in Tatlayoko and she start to dry. Really nice and dry. And she pick some saskatoon and dry for winter time.

One time she had some cattle. She got about ten head of cattle, I think. You know she make hay by hand, using a butcher knife. She make pretty near enough hay for winter time too, for ten head of cattle and one horse.

She build a little cabin. And he stay inside and it's open on top. Pretty tough livin'. I guess she don't feel the cold.

One time she can't make hay no more. Hurt her hand. Pretty near broke off her thumb. So she ask Alex Graham, and Alex she feed for him that cow. And she had to camp out all winter underneath some spruce. Three feet of snow, still she camp out. Fifty below, still going to camp out.

You know from that fire, that first fire she make, going to thaw down to the dirt. She sleep in a warm place over there. Pretty dusty, look pretty dirty. You know, never comb his hair, just tangled up really. Just spring time, maybe about May, it start getting warm, he wash his hair. She never wash his face.

You know sometime she come to Tatla Lake on a cold day, she got lots of blanket on top of the saddle horse. You know, just after she married off her daughter, that time it's pretty hard living. After Mary Jane was 14 she left him, so Lillie just by himself.

Everybody go for priest at Redstone church house. Chief call for Lillie. Ask, "Do you want this guy to marry your daughter?"

"That guy, he's too black. No good. Going to spoil my daughter." So they didn't get married. Later the priest, Father Hennessy, he marry Henry and Mary Jane at Anaham.

So Henry don't like Lillie very much. "No," he said. "Lillie, he's pretty dirty."

Lillie not dirty. Just don't wash. Sometimes he wash. Nice looking woman, have a bath. Winter time never comb his hair. Just tangled up. Look like she not going to comb it anymore. But she wash and comb it a little bit. Pretty soon she make it straight. She got long hair.

90 *Chiwid*

FIRE ON TOP
OF THE ICE

RANDOLPH MULVAHILL *spent a lot of time on horseback in Chezacut country where he was born. Trails fanned out in all directions from the broad meadows of the upper Chilcotin River valley, and Randolph knew most of them.*

I was out hunting horses on the mountain by Chezacut Lake, and I could hear what sounded like a kid crying. I was positive it was a kid crying. My horse was nervous because he didn't know what it was. He tossed his head and rolled the bit in his mouth. Finally I had to get off him to quiet him down. And sure enough, I could hear a kid crying.

I thought something was haywire, so I got back on my horse and rode down this trail to where the sound was coming from. I honestly didn't know that trail was there. I saw horse tracks on the trail, and little kid tracks.

FACING PAGE: *Ollie Nukalow*

Chiwid 91

As soon as the kid sees me, it let out a hell of a shriek and crawled under a log.

Well, what the hell are you going to do? The horse I was riding was green and not that well broke to pack a kid on, so I thought the best thing to do was not to do anything.

Horse tracks went down the trail, so I thought there must be something to it. I went like hell down the trail, and catches up to Chiwid. She was leading her saddle horse and three packhorses . . .

She didn't really know me when I caught up to her. I said the little kid was crying, and I was kind of worried about her.

She said: "All the time he do that way. He cry and cry. After a while he come."

The kid didn't want to ride one of the horses. Wanted to walk, but couldn't keep up. They were coming down to Shillaker's store at Chezacut.

Then Chiwid wanted to know who I was. I said: "Well, Charlie Mulvahill's boy."

Then she remembered me: "Oh yeah . . . a long time ago."

One winter Bob Smith and I were driving some cattle from Towdystan to Anahim Lake and we saw Chiwid. It was cold, about 16 below and we were driving some cattle around the end of this little lake. We stayed with Fred Engebretson all night and the next morning picked the cattle up all along the road.

We got out there on the lake and see this old Indian woman. I knew her from a long time before. She was going to get her horse which was staked out in the meadow. She had moccasin rubbers on, but no socks or moccasins on. She was barefooted.

As we got up to her, Bob stopped and talked to her a little bit. She takes off one moccasin rubber and dumps the snow out of it and puts it back on. Then she puts the other leg up like this and dumps the snow out of it.

Bob says, "Where are you going?" And she says, "Going to get my saddle horse. And we went on up to the holding grounds. We were staying there with Tommy Holte. I says to Bob, "Holy God that woman's tough!" And he says, "She sure as hell is."

She was barefooted in those moccasin rubbers and it was 16 below when we left Fred Engebretson's at Towdystan.

ANDREW SQUINAS, *born in 1925 at Ulkatcho Village, moved to Anahim Lake where his paternal grandfather, Domas Squinas had a ranch. He remembers the time Chiwid camped overnight at Geese Point on Anahim Lake.*

One winter is 40 below. She was fishing out at Little Anahim Point. In 40 below, he stay down on the ice. He sleep right there too. Cut up little dry willow brush beside him. Pack 'em up. Got little fire on top of the ice.

He got fishing hole in the ice. He stay overnight. Next day, he go back to Towdystan. But he got no home. No tent up there.

Used to be he got cow. Nine or ten head. I know he got one horse. He keep him all the time. Then after, he tie him up down his place, one week. That horse he die. He don't drink water. He eat grass alright, but he don't drink water. That horse he die.

Chiwid, just like some animal, some kind of dog, something like that.

He live at Kleena Kleene most of the time. Sometime, he want fish. Get on a horse, come this way. Sometime, he want moose. He go out in the bush. Then he stay there. I don't know how he kill a moose. He got no gun. I don't know how he do. But maybe somebody help him get the moose.

BAPTISTE ELKINS *married Chiwid's younger sister, Madeline Palmantier and they made their home at Anahim Lake. On one occasion Chiwid stayed in the house with the Elkins family for about a week. It was very unusual for her to stay indoors that long.*

Chiwid set on ice, fishing. No bait. Just a straight hook. Just a little bit of a fire in the willow brush. Me and my son Freddie were hauling wood when we see him.

Next morning, we go down with a sleigh. Walk right up to him.

"You know my house?" I says: "You go there. Feed you if you are hungry."

We get home three hours later, and he was there, set alongside the stove . . .

My wife give him half the fish. He don't cut open. Just cut in half. Put in pot. Eat guts and all.

WILLIE SULIN (1918–1994) *was the son of Old Sulin, a Tsilhqot'in man, and Ellie Stillas, a Southern Carrier from Ulkatcho Village. Willie trapped, hunted, guided and cowboyed all over the country and lived his whole life at Towdystan, just a few miles up the road from Fred Engebretson.*

One time, when it was 50 below, I was chasing cattle for Fred Brink. When we got down by Cariboo Flats, I see a little smoke coming out by the side of the road. Lillie Skinner was there.

"What you doing, Lillie?" I tell him.

"Shit, I'm cold," he said.

It was after Christmas when we chased those cattle down for Fred Brink. Gee that was cold. Lillie was leading his horse and chasing his cows, too. Heading down to her brother Scotty's place, at Clearwater Lake.

I told him: "Lillie, you all right?"

"I'm okay," he said. "Just warm up myself."

Holy shit, he only got a little fire.

Sometimes, Lillie used to camp down the road by Towdystan, and hunt squirrels on the other side. I see him there.

"How's Lillie?" I tell him.

"Not bad. I'm alright. I got good axe," he tell me.

Some winters, it was so cold I thought he was going to freeze to death. One time he came in that old house we used to live in.

"Willie?"

"Yeah," I told him.

He told me, "I get cold."

He put lots of wood in the heater, and made a big fire. Jeeze, it was really hot and I didn't want to stay in there. I went out. My wife Lucy got mad at Lillie. He told him: "Fucking warm here. That's too warm. No way."

Lillie just stayed two hours. Then he went out again, leading that old horse. He tied him up in the meadow, and camped out for the night.

It was cold outside, but in the house he couldn't get warm. Really funny. Outside he was okay. Cold-blooded, I guess . . .

One time, just the other side, I found Lillie's kid, Mary Jane. He was about two years old. I guess Lillie's horse took off, and he went to look for it. That kid, he go to sleep right there. Where one road goes through. The kid was there.

"Hey kid," I told him.

"Mommy took off," he said. "He chase the horse."

There was a blanket right there, and the kid had been sleeping. So, I took off, and after a while, I found Lillie way on top of the hill.

"I lost my horse," he say.

"I can get it for you," I tell him. "Go back to your daughter."

Not too long, I found the horse in a meadow, just behind the hill. I led the horse down, back to Lillie's camp. Lillie wasn't there yet, but that kid was still there, asleep on top of the blanket.

I don't think Lillie was crazy. All his life he was like that.

EDWARD SILL *grew up in Anahim Lake country, but when he was 12 years old he was adopted by his half-brother, Eagle Lake Henry.*

When Mary Jane was a little kid, Chiwid take him to Anahim Lake Stampede. Somebody ask him, "What you do with your daughter?" He say, "I tie him up in the camp."

Just like a dog, he tie him up in the camp. He said he leave some water with him and tie him up in the camp. Mary Jane just a little kid.

AL ELSEY came to Bella Coola from the Okanagan in 1951, and met his wife Julie. They bought the Talchako Lodge at Stuie in the mid fifties, and ran it for more than a dozen years until the late sixties.

We always went out in the fall, consistently, between November 15 to 25 every year, once the lodge was closed for the season. In those days, it took two full days to get to Williams Lake.

We'd always see Chiwid. She was often camped at Clearwater Lake, by Kleena Kleene. Just camped on the hillside, it wasn't even level. Another placed she camped, at the east end of Tatla Lake, up from Chilanko Forks.

She had many horses that always died. People'd give her a horse, or she'd get a horse some place, and they'd just die. She'd tie them up to a tree and they hardly had anything to eat.

We'd often stop overnight at Tatla Lake and we'd talk about Chiwid with Betty Linder. Her husband Fred knew her better than anybody, from a white point of view.

He had a lot of good things to say about her. He liked her, though he used to get a little mad at her because she wouldn't use any common sense on some things.

One time I saw her, it was 40-plus below at Clearwater Lake. I just happened to glance over and saw the smoke. Blue smoke, quite a bit of it, drifting around there. And I saw this funny looking shape. You wouldn't call it a tent. Sort of rags, not plastic. Material hung over. Maybe parts of a tent. She had this little place she could go into.

She was sitting just out in front, by this tiny little fire which was making a lot of smoke. It wasn't much of a fire. You couldn't keep much warm, except your hands a bit. And she was singing. Sort of humming. And she was moving a little, back and forth. Moving with the rhythm of it, up and down like that. I don't have a picture of her face except she was old then. She gave you the impression of being old.

She was camped on the hillside past Baptiste Dester's, just as you start to climb the hill on the old road there. She was quite a ways from the creek, up above the road. It wasn't even flat. Here she was sitting there, so I stopped and got out and went over there.

It was cold, cold. It was so cold that I believe she was suffering from hypothermia, because of that sound she was making. When I spoke to her, she made some noises. You couldn't really understand what she was saying.

I don't remember her even looking right at me. She was all covered over with a whole lot of raggy things, and I'll never forget she had some dried squawfish there. Hard, hard squawfish hanging up. A whole bunch of them. Dried squawfish are harder than rock. I've dried some. If they weren't hard from drying, they would be from frozen. There was no other evidence of food around, though I'm sure she had something there.

I'd seen her before, but never got really close to her. But this time I stopped. It was cold, and my wife stayed in the truck. I went over and walked down. I thought: "Here she is." At the time I wondered: "Why would she live like this?" I didn't know much about her then. I got inquisitive and started asking questions.

Of course Fred and Betty Linder supplied me with most of my answers. The Grahams were pretty good. If they didn't see Chiwid around, they'd go and look for her. Fred would find her and take her stuff. Sometimes he'd take hay for her horse. Poor old Fred. He was sort of a half outcast in the Graham family in a way. He married into the Grahams and then he had a drinking problem, poor old Fred. I liked Fred, to be honest with you. He was a likeable sort of guy. A character, maybe a bit of a bum. He was good to her.

I think probably Fred Linder, and his wife Betty, were very responsible for Chiwid managing to survive as long she did under those conditions. Because let me tell you, those were the toughest conditions. You wouldn't believe.

They built her a cabin at Tatla Lake. I think it's still standing, but she'd never go into the thing, they say, because of her background. Because of the way she was beat up by her husband . . .

Al Elsey skinning a caribou.

Nobody cared for her really much except Betty Linder and Fred. They did their best to keep her alive in the condition that she chose for herself. They had reasonable respect for her choice. They wanted to try and change it, of course, but they discovered after years they couldn't change it. That they'd just have to accept her the way she was.

When I came to Bella Coola in September of 1951, the Ulkatcho Indians used to camp in the trees next to the Cedar Inn where the Bella Coola townsite is today. That's where I met Ollie [Chiwid's brother].

Not long after I was there, Ollie came over to the house and asked me if I had any work he could do. He said he needed enough money to buy a box of snuff, a comb and a pair of gloves. The total cost was just over two bucks.

I didn't have any work for him to do, but I loaned him the money. Two or three dollars was almost half a day's pay in those days.

He said: "When I come down in the spring-time, I'll pay you."

I just trusted the guy.

In the spring of 1952, there was a shortage of hay in Anahim Lake, and Ollie brought a bunch of his horses down to the valley. That was fairly common in those days. The first thing he did, when they camped and made their fire over in the big spruce trees across from the co-op store, Ollie came to the house and he paid me.

"I owe you," he said.

We became really good friends after that. As the years went by he worked for me a little bit. When we got the lodge, he came up and split fence posts for me one year. Ollie was a tremendous worker. When he said something, he meant it.

A year later, at Red Hill cabin, Ollie took me moose hunting for the first time. That was the year the Bella Coola road was being built, and it wasn't finished yet. We drove from Bella Coola as far as the top of the first set of switchbacks, and backpacked about two and a half miles the rest of the way to Red Hill. Ollie and his wife, Aggie Sill, were camped there at Young Creek.

Ollie smelled our smoke and came down and offered to rent us horses and take us hunting.

The next day we started out and rode four horses up the mountain. We took a shortcut up the West Branch through a shmozzle of dead-fall. We didn't get to East Fork until 2:30 in the afternoon. We got up just below timberline and shot two moose. By the time we got them gutted it was about 5 o'clock. It was eleven miles back to Red Hill camp. We got home about 10 o'clock.

The next day, we got the pack horses and went back up. But they were slow. We were slow getting going in the morning, and didn't get there until about 3 o'clock. Then Ollie said – I'll never forget this – "Well, tea time!"

We had no tea. We didn't have anything with us. I thought he was joking. We're at timberline, and all there is to burn is some short scrubby willow brush and a few balsams. So Ollie breaks off a bunch of dead sticks and pretty soon he's got a little fire going. Just a tiny little fire.

He's got this little sack, a grey-looking flour sack tied on behind his saddle. He takes it out and he's got four bully beef cans, with the lids not cut right off.

"Cup?" he says.

Also in the sack he's got a can of tobacco, half a pound of Player's tobacco. So he takes his bandanna off his neck, spreads it out on the grass, takes his tobacco, dumps it in the bandanna, and ties it up so it won't spill.

Then, he goes down to this little tiny creek and washes out the tin can, fills it with water, and sticks it on the fire. Pretty soon it's boiling.

Then, he reaches in his shirt pocket and he takes out a handful of loose tea. Throws it in there.

"Tea time," he says.

So we have a cup of tea. Then he says to me: "Soogar?"

I says: "You're kidding!"

Then he laughed, and over on the other side in his shirt pocket, he's got some lumped sugar.

JOY GRAHAM came to the Chilcotin in 1935 to take a job house-keeping and never left. She married Bill Graham, the oldest son of Tatla Lake Ranch owner Bob Graham and sister to Betty Linder, owner of the store at Tatla Lake. Among her many duties around the ranch, Joy also worked in the store.

Chiwid was a strange woman. She didn't mix with the Indians hardly at all. They thought she was strange and they sort of shunned her because of it. We'd see her at the store in Tatla Lake once in a while.

She didn't have much meat on her. She was pretty skinny. You might say she just existed.

She had squirrels and she'd bring the pelts into the store and trade them for groceries. Betty always gave her more for them than their value. She tried to give her all the necessities.

In winter time she'd come into the store and it was cold. She had every stitch of clothes she owned on. What really got me was her feet. They'd be in moccasins and they were frozen stiff. And she'd walk into the store and these frozen moccasins would go "clack, clack, clack" across the floor.

It didn't seem to bother her feet any. As far as I know she never froze her feet. But she had those moccasins on and they were just as stiff as boards.

JOYCE ROBERTSON was a friend and admirer of Chiwid. In 1953, she and her husband Phil and their daughter Catherine moved to Tatla Lake. Phil took a job as a mechanic for the Graham Ranch and Joyce worked occasionally in the store.

One time I remember Chiwid came down the side of the hill above the store. She was riding her horse and had a couple quarters of moose tied on the horse behind. She wanted to know if anyone wanted to buy this meat.

Well, it was summer time and the meat was all pretty well haywire, rotten by then. Fly-blown. But Betty paid her for it. She said: "Oh well, we'll feed it to the chickens." They didn't want to waste it.

Betty was always good about Lillie. Kind of looked after her, making sure she had enough to eat.

Betty would go looking for her periodically to make sure she had supplies. Betty and Fred would get in the car on a Sunday and go look for her. If they couldn't find her they'd just ask people where she was at.

I TAKE HIM
FROM COYOTE

PHIL ROBERTSON *first went to Tatla Lake in 1946 to feed cattle for his cousin Alex Graham. Then he went to work for Bill Graham driving his bulldozer. Bill offered Phil a job to work the machine on the highway to Anahim Lake, and in 1953 Phil and his wife* JOYCE *decided to move to Tatla Lake.*

JOYCE: When we first went to Tatla Lake, Chiwid had a horse. Maybe a couple of years later, something happened to her horse. It was so old and everything.

Fred Linder was coming up the old Bear Head Hill Road that used to come from Chilanko along the edge of the hill. It used to cross at the bottom of Tatla Lake and go up through the draw there. Bear Head Gulch we called it.

Lillie was camped out at the bottom there when Fred came along

FACING PAGE: *The Tatla Lake "store" at Redstone Flats, where Betty and Fred Linder would exchange groceries from their car for furs. Donald Ekks is third from the right.*

and she was in a great fuss. Oh, so upset. There was a bear stalking her horse, but the horse had died and the bear wanted to eat on it. But she didn't want the bear eating on that horse. She had this old .22 and she was going to shoot this bear.

So Fred got the .22 and lined it up on the bear, and pulled the trigger. Nothing happened, just "click." So I guess that was the end of that. He didn't shoot any bear. Not with a gun like that . . .

The government used to give Lillie an allotment every month for groceries. Betty Linder was to look after it for her, and make sure she got food. We used to take groceries to her. A little box of everything. There was a certain amount of money and Betty would put in what she thought she'd use. One time she put in a bar of Lifebuoy soap.

The next time we went, I found her Lifebuoy soap lying on the ground. She must have chucked it. The paper was ripped off, and there were teeth marks on it. I guess she didn't know what it was. I don't think she washed very much.

She didn't use all the groceries Betty sent out. I know she had to have her tea, sugar and flour. She liked lots of sugar. She made tea with no milk, but lots of sugar. Maybe two or three teaspoons.

PHIL: One time, Lillie was camped over by Hook Lake. Late 1953 or early 1954. It was terribly cold that winter, about 55 or maybe 60 below, and lots of snow. I think she had a tent that time.

Alex Graham was riding over that way and he came upon her camp. She had a deer strung up in quarters, hanging from the limb of a jackpine tree, and he says, "You catch'em mowich, Lillie?"

"No," she says, "I no catch him."

He said: "How you get him then?"

"Well," she says, "Coyote kill him. Me, I take him from coyote."

That's how she got her deer. The coyotes run it down on the lake.

JOYCE and PHIL *moved to Puntzi in 1957 where Phil worked as a heavy duty equipment operator for ten years at Puntzi Mountain air base. When the base closed, Joyce became the school teacher. In those years, Chiwid lived in a number of seasonal camps, travelling between Kleena Kleene and Redstone.*

JOYCE: Our daughter was swimming at Pyper Lake one day. She had gone there with these other kids and their father, and while they were there, Lillie came over waving her hands. "Bear eat all my fish!" she was yelling. She was drying suckers at the mouth of the creek there.

The father of the other girls said, "Oh she's crazy, don't pay any attention to her. Come on, let's go home." But when Louise got home she was all upset and said, "There's a bear getting all Lillie's fish that she's drying."

So Phil got his gun and we all went up to see if we could find the bear that was bothering her, because she was very upset. So when we got there Phil took off to look around for the bear, and we stayed in camp with her. Pretty soon, Lillie says: "Come, come. You want to see my little kitty, my puppy too?"

The kids got interested and wanted to see this "kitty."

She showed us this wash tub which was upside down. She lifted it up and here was this little mink in there. She had it tied by the hind leg to a stick in the ground with some store string. It hissed and made quite a fuss when it saw us.

She pulled on the string and out come this mink. It hissed at us, but she could handle it. It was her pet. She'd stroke that mink and kept saying to it: "My little kitty."

It didn't seem to mind. It was diving around here and turning around, and would disappear into her clothes. Then it would stick its head up and hiss.

She must have spent a lot of time with it. It liked her. She was quite proud of her little pet.

PHIL: When I got back from looking for the bear, I asked her, "How you catch'em mink, Lillie?" She said, "I put bacon . . ." Then she showed how she had the washtub turned upside down, propped up with a stick about a foot long, with a string tied to it. Then she waited and waited until that mink got in there, then she pulled the string and had him.

But I never asked how she got that mink after she had it in there, how she managed to catch him and get the string on his foot. I always wondered how she could she get in there and get that mink without it coming out. Your arm is thicker than the mink's body, and a mink can move pretty damn fast. He'd chew your fingers up before you knew what hit them.

The Indians out there, years ago, if they got a horse that was too tough, they'd feed him "post hay" for a while. Just tie him up and leave him there. No water, no hay, or anything. Just tie him up. Pretty soon he gets a little weak.

Maybe take him out and try and ride him. Once they rode him and got him tamed down enough, then give him a little more hay. Then ride him a little bit more. That way you can't get hurt.

Maybe she did that with the mink . . .

One time, Hank Law and Carl Conan were out riding, and they came upon Lillie's camp. They looked and there was fresh snow on the ground, but they couldn't find her anywhere. So, Hank gave out a beller, "Hey Lillie!" There was no answer, so Hank hollered some more.

Pretty soon a bunch of clothing under the snow erupted and old Chiwid sat up. She was there. They woke her up. Of course when the blankets came alive, the horses did too. The horses took off on a jump and it pretty near piled Conan. Old Hank laughed.

CARM PURJUE *came to Tatla Lake with her husband Will in 1953 to run the boarding house for students attending the school. She ran the boarding house for eight years and spent many years working in the general store for Betty Linder.*

The kids all used to say that Chiwid must have a guardian angel to keep her alive.

She was scared of the dogs at Tatla Lake. When she'd come to the store, instead of coming up the road, she'd walk along that ridge. When she got above the store, she'd come down.

EDWARD SILL *was 12 when his father, Thomas Sill, died and his older brother Joe brought him to visit their half brother Eagle Lake Henry. Henry, who had no children of his own, took a liking to his younger sibling and invited him to stay. Edward eventually married Jenny Lulua, daughter of Tommy Lulua, who lived across the Chilko River from Henry, and he remained in the Eagle Lake country.*

Lillie Skinner had lots of cattle. First time I meet him was at Willie George's place at Skinner Meadow. Chiwid got some cattle and horses then. I don't know where he put them. Pretty soon take them up to Scotty Gregg's place, this side Mack Dester's at Kleena Kleene. Chiwid stay up on the hill, this side.

One time a lynx come into Chiwid's camp. Pretty soon he catch him, right beside the campfire. Set trap for him and catch him right there. Chiwid killed that lynx and skin it. Then when he stretched it, he twisted it half way around. His tail right in front.

Fred Linder used to own the store at Tatla Lake, and he bought that lynx from Chiwid. Everytime Fred come into the store he'd say, "Ever see that kind of lynx?" I get fooled. I see lots of lynx, but I get fooled.

One day I ride saddle horse from Eagle Lake to Tatla Lake. About 35 miles. I want to go to Anahim Lake. Somebody said more money for lynx fur and that kind of thing up there. Tatla Lake just old Bob Graham ranch house over there. No cafe, nothing. Just old ranch house and a little cabin where the Indian stay. I come over there. Chiwid stay there at that cabin.

I look for ride most of the day. Pretty soon I come back. I see he got that cabin nice and warm in there. I tell Chiwid I try catch ride to Anahim Lake. It cold at night. I come in. Just about freeze. Half cold.

Chiwid, he sleep that side of wall. Little heater stove in middle. Pretty soon I say, "I bring my pack in?"

"Sure bring everything in."

I got one lynx inside my sleeping bag. As soon as I bring him in, he go this way, start sniffing the air. "Lynx!" he say.

Jeez he scare me that time. How the hell he know I got lynx inside that bag? Inside all double bag. As soon as I bring him in. Jeez he scare me. I just about run out that time. How the hell he know? He got a good nose. Maybe grizzly. Maybe half crazy or something.

So I go back out. Try to catch a ride some more that night. I can't get a ride. After dark I come back again. He say, "My bed a little bit small. If a little more big you sleep with me."

But I look at him. I never say nothing. He got a little bed like that, you know. I stay the other side. Just lay right beside the stove.

Doreen Seaforth, *daughter of Julianna Setah and granddaughter of Chiwid, spent her early years in the Tatlayoko/Eagle Lake area. Then when she was old enough to go to school, she and her brother Norman were sent to St. Joseph's residential school near Williams Lake. For many years after that, they never saw their parents from September until June.*

Dad fed cattle for Ken Moore over at Skinner Meadow, and we lived right there. Granny lived nearby too. Dad built a little shack for her to live in. Granny didn't like us kids to come over. She always used to send us away. I think she was afraid we'd steal her candy.

In the summer, we used to go up to the Potato Mountains. Granny used to come too, and pick lots of berries and dry them. There used to be a big gathering up there, and a big rodeo. I don't remember the rodeo. I was so busy looking for berries. Everybody from Eagle Lake was there, half of Nemiah, and people from Redstone all came to dig wild potatoes. Our whole family would go up for two weeks at a time. We'd dry some deer meat as well. Granny used to come too. I remember she had a horse with a foal.

Then we'd come down and go fencing for someone.

In the fall we'd go back up again to hunt deer. Granny came with us then too. I think she'd be the first one to shoot the deer. In the winter time, Granny used to hunt squirrels. She'd go out just about every day. All she had was a single-shot .22.

All the white oldtimers knew her really well.

When my brother Norman and I were old enough to go to school, we were sent to the mission in Williams Lake. We hardly saw our parents or Granny after that. Mom and Dad moved to Redstone, then they went to Nemiah. Eventually they settled down at Big Creek and built a cabin at Fletcher Lake. When we were at the mission, we never saw our parents from September until June.

Granny had six or seven cattle when we were at Eagle Lake. She used to follow them from meadow to meadow and cut hay for them with a knife. A few starved over the winter, so I guess her brother, Scotty, decided to sell them for her. She had sixteen or seventeen cows by the time they were sold.

Granny had a tent, but she never had it up. She just kept it in her belongings pile, with a tarp over it. She always built a little windbreak, two or three feet high. She just had a tarp to cover her, and her blankets hardly consisted of anything. But you never saw her sitting there with her teeth rattling.

Basically, she lived off the land. She was really quite healthy. She was well into her 60s, and her teeth were still really good.

Later, after I was married, we saw Granny camping on the other side of Tatla Lake, not too far from the store. We were going to the Anahim Lake Stampede. She must have killed a deer, because she had a hind quarter of deer leg hanging up. She must have been there for quite a while. She told us she was staying for the summer.

She was on foot. She had no horse in those days. She just had enough stuff that she could pack around with her.

I went to talk to her, and she said she was going to take somebody to court for stealing her husband.

When she got old, she ended up in the hospital for a week. She didn't like the food. She called the doctor "Englishman who stole all my money." She always called the whitemen "Scotchman."

After she was released from the hospital, they were going to put her in an old folks home, but she didn't want to go. They took her back to Stone. She wanted to go to Eagle Lake, but I guess she couldn't get a ride.

Everybody, in a way, thought Granny was weird. But in a way they were proud of her too . . .

Mary Jane was 14 or 15 when she shacked up with the first guy [Tommy Jack] from Redstone. Then she went with Henry Lulua.

Mom didn't want her to marry Henry. She had a big fight with Mary Jane. They were all sitting around the stove, and pretty soon all the wood was flying. Granny said she didn't care. She came in and cracked Mom with a hide tanning stick. My mom didn't want Mary Jane to marry Henry . . .

The last time we went to the Williams Lake Stampede with a team and wagon was in 1963 or '64. The wagon road from the Chilcotin River to Nemiah Valley used to take four days in a wagon.

After the Williams Lake Stampede, everybody went to the Chilko Bridge and camped for the summer. We caught fish there.

I'd like to go back to the Potato Mountains some day, but I don't know where to find the wild potatoes any more. It's been so long.

IRENE BLISS *still tends the fires at her home at Willow Springs Ranch where she has lived more than 60 years with her husband Bill. Her son Walt has taken over the ranching duties now. An old hand crank gas pump still stands in front of their house as a memento of former times.*

Another time when Fred and Betty delivered groceries to Chiwid, they had old Mrs. Krause with them. When they got there, Chiwid was eating a half-cooked squirrel she had roasted over her fire. The blood from the squirrel was running down from the corners of her mouth.

Poor old Mrs. Krause had to throw up. She couldn't stand it . . .

Chiwid mostly came down past our place at Willow Springs in the summer, at salmon time. There used to be lots of Indian camps at Siwash Bridge, on the hill there across the river.

It used to be a lovely place to go. The horses with the bells on all over, and these Indian fires and camps and fish drying in every direction.

RITA LULUA MELDRUM *is the second oldest daughter of Mary Jane Lulua, Chiwid's youngest daughter. While Rita was growing up near Henry's Crossing, her grandmother often camped nearby.*

Chiwid was my favorite grandmother, and I was her favorite granddaughter. She was unique because she used to live outside. Nobody else did at 50 below. She stayed quite close to our house.

When she lived outside she just had a little campfire. But when she came to live with us inside the house, the house would be boiling. She always thought it was cold. For some reason, she always got it reversed. She could never get it hot enough. If we had the windows open, she'd close them. If we tried to open the door, she'd close it again.

Granny used to tell stories, but I can't remember them much now.

My dad [Henry Lulua] didn't really trust her. We were told not to go and see her. But we used to sneak to go see her anyway.

She just drank out of little tin cans, and I loved it. I thought it was really neat. We had cups in the house and Granma had tin cans to drink out of. We used to drink out of her tin cans and our parents used to get mad at us. But I thought it was neat.

Granny travelled around. She just packed her stuff from one place to another on foot. My parents thought she was crazy, but I didn't think she was crazy at all. I thought she was really spiritual. Everybody else thought she was just nuts.

Every time Dad would go out hunting or something, all of a sudden Granny would sniff the air: "Oh your dad just shot a deer today."

And I'd say: "Really?" And I'd run back to the camp and tell my mom and my aunt Jenny.

And she'd go: "Ah! That's just lies. She's filling your head with lies."

And you know, dad would come back home half an hour later with a deer or something.

She was always right on, I thought. I knew she made sense, but everybody told me: "Don't listen to her. Don't listen to her."

I used to remember Granny moving away and coming back again. I don't know how often she spent time with us. I always remember the times she was around, which wasn't very often.

Granny didn't like my dad. She always thought my dad was wrong for my mom. I always thought she was a sweet lady.

I don't remember Granny using a gun to hunt. She always used little strings to catch animals. She lived outside and survived.

The elders told us kids to stay away from Granny. They said she was really bad because she got spiritual powers. Even my Aunt Jenny said she had bad spiritual powers.

STONE
RANCHERIE

MACK SQUINAS *is recognized as the spiritual leader of the Ulkatcho community in Anahim Lake. Once a respected trapper and guide/outfitter, Mack continues to offer leadership in his role as an elder.*

She never came into this rancherie [Anahim Lake Reserve] and talked to people. If she came, she camped way back in the top of the hill some place. She live out, hunting in the woods by herself. Set rabbit snares. Caught lots of rabbits, and she smoked them. She don't cut them. Just cut open their guts and hang up in the smoke. Smoke them dry as a bone. Pack around all summer. Any time she wants some rabbit, just chop up and boil it and eat.

That's all she lived on. Just rabbits and fish. She don't go to the store to buy anything. Those days, there was no welfare, no old age

114   *Chiwid*

pension, nothing. That's the way she lived. Move out in the woods, all winter too. Snow don't matter.

She never got sick. Must be she got some medicine out of the woods.

RANDOLPH MULVAHILL *remembers Chiwid and Alec Jack from his early boyhood, growing up in Chezacut.*

Alec Jack, I knew him well. He worked for me, and was a really good old Indian. You hired him, and you had a good man. He'd do anything. You give him a wild horse to ride, and he'd ride it. He was a good cowboy, and knew what to do.

A damn good hand with a horse, and a good bronc rider, anytime. He wasn't afraid to ride wild horses because he was such a good rider. He could ride any kind of horse. He'd go on them big beef drives to Ashcroft. Then he could turn around and still mow hay and stuff, too.

When he was an old man, Alec Jack comes out of Nemiah Valley riding a big snorty bronc. The horse bucks on the frozen ground and fell, rolling right on top of him.

This dislocates Alec's leg at the ball joint. The leg stuck right out sideways, and he laid there all night with nobody around.

Next day, this Indian come by on horseback and he seen him. He said: "His leg stuck out like this, and I pick him up and put him back like the other one. Jeez, he holler like hell," he said.

They got him into town, and they had to send the poor old bugger into Vancouver. They operated on him and straighted it out. When he came back, one leg was shorter than the other. So, the Indians used to laugh. They'd say: "He's good sidehill country. He can go one way around the mountain." Laugh like hell over it.

God, that guy had to be tough. He laid out there all night on the frozen ground, and he was an old man. Never took pneumonia or nothing. Endurance of that kind is hard to believe. A normal person would have died.

FACING PAGE: *Chiwid in her camp at Stone Rancherie.*

ILLA GRAHAM *knew Chiwid at Towdystan when she was a young girl, then later at Tatla Lake after she married Alex Graham.*

At one time, she was a lady you could probably take into your confidence. But as she got older, she got withdrawn into a state where she didn't want to be around people. You couldn't get close to her. She was afraid of everybody. When she got really old, they wanted to move her into a cabin. They took her to the Stone rancherie because her daughter lived there. They had a house for her there.

Her daughter, Julianna, said it took months before they could get her in the house. Even in the cold weather. Finally, she got so she'd go in the house and stay in the house and cook in the house.

She lived for years and years, just camping out. That's why they called her Chiwid. She was like a little bird, like the ptarmigans that would sleep right in the snow. That's what she used to do, too. No one knew how she did it.

JOYCE ROBERTSON *never lost her admiration and respect for Chiwid, even after she left the Chilcotin and moved to McLeese Lake.*

The last time we saw her, she was camped at Stone Reserve along the fence there. It was about 1974 or 1975, and we were going out to Nemiah Valley.

After we had gone through the reserve, we saw all this junk scattered around. It looked like a camp, and I remember thinking: "This looks like one of Chiwid's camps." And, by golly, it was. Sure enough, there she was, with all her little things that she used to have around her camp.

So, we stopped to talk to her, and she smiled and was happy to see us.

We had four boys with us and told them to stay in the Travel-All because we didn't want Lillie to get upset. She knew us, but she was shy. But they couldn't stay in. Those four kids came trooping out. Lillie clammed up and wouldn't say much after that.

That's the last time we saw her. They had already moved her down to Stone, and she stayed the last days of her life there. But she wasn't inside. She was outside, just off the edge of the reserve, in a little patch of trees beside the road. The same as always, living outside.

Once WILF HODGSON *sold his trucking business in 1963, he and his wife Drew bought the Chilcotin Lodge at Riske Creek, which they ran until the mid seventies. It was then he saw Chiwid for the last time.*

Willie George and Julianna Setah were feeding cattle for Jack Durrell that winter, at the Wineglass Ranch near Riske Creek. We owned the Chilcotin Lodge at Riske Creek at the time, and used to see Chiwid quite a bit. She spent the winter camped by the road near Hance's Timber. No tent or anything.

Delmer Jasper and I went and looked at her camp one time. We didn't see any blankets, just a pile that looked like rags. There was a .22 rifle and a little kitten. And a few squirrel skins. That's all that seemed to be there. I didn't see any food or anything.

It was one of those really cold winters. I don't know where she was when we came by. Maybe she could see us coming and took off or something.

I talked to old Tommy Lulua one time, and he said Chiwid was just like an animal. She'd be sitting right out in the open, in the rain and cold, and he said the steam would be coming off her, just like an animal.

Any time I saw her when she was at her camp, she always had just a little bit of a fire. I don't know how old she was. The last time I saw her at Riske Creek in 1969, she didn't look like an old woman then.

CHARLIE QUILT *knew Chiwid when he was a young man, and then again in his later years, when they were both blind.*

Chiwid my girl friend too, before. Bull Canyon he camped out. I comin' along. I stay one night with him. A long time ago.

That time he got a horse, he got a pack horse. He alright for a while like that, by God.

He stay out of town all the time. Sometimes it cold, by God. Deep snow too, by God. It freeze up his leg one time. Packing the wood in, by God, and he got wet. It froze in here on his thigh, by God. He's alright after he thawed out.

Sometime I got a chainsaw, I got a team, I haul some wood for him, by God. It so cold for him too. By God, I got to come in. He still stay outside in 60 below. He stays right by the camp. By the fire. Yeah, I make wood for him, by God. One big load of wood I haul it in for him. By God, I can't stand it no more. Too cold.

Then he went blind, just like me. He had a hard time packing wood. Bark go in his eye, that's why he went blind.

That's why he can't live by himself no more. He stay over here. Katie and Zaloway they watch him for a long time. He can't help himself, he's blind. That's why he come in. Stay with Katie and Zaloway. Maybe four or five years before he die.

LOUISA JEFF *lived all her life in the east Chilcotin area around Riske Creek. After Chiwid moved to Stone, Louisa visited her occasionally.*

A long time ago, Chiwid make a fire and stay outside all winter. At Stone, he do that. He sleeping outside. Just like an animal, you know, he sleep outside. I don't think he got sick living like that. Just a small fire, he do that. Not very big.

Sometimes, I talk to him at Stone. He said: "I don't want to stay with somebody. People too much a-talk."

He don't like people. He usually can't stay with people. He go by himself, he likes it. When he got too old, somebody look after him. Bring him inside. He die.

Katie Quilt looked after him at Stone until he died.

DONALD EKKS *never received any formal schooling and has spent his whole life in close touch with the traditions of his culture. One of these traditions is to pass on knowledge by word of mouth, and*

Donald is something of a spokesman for the history of his people.

Chiwid never get sick. Just one time she get pneumonia. Not too long ago. She stay in the hospital ten or fifteen days. After that she never stay outside any more.

She live at Stone Reserve after that, in a house. Then one day she get sick, and she die the next day. She was pretty old. Way past 80.

HELENA MYERS *was one of the people who gave Chiwid the freedom to live the life she chose. Sharing the produce from her garden was one way she helped Chiwid survive against all odds.*

Chiwid enjoyed the outdoors. She used to stay across the road from my house at Stone. Just camp down there. Sometimes it was 40 below out there. She'd just have a little fire. One time her face was frozen when they brought her inside the house.

I first met Chiwid at Nemiah, sometime after she had split up with her husband, Alec Jack. She never stayed in a house. She was staying around Eagle Lake and was making moccasins and selling them.

The way Chiwid could stay outside, she was probably dreaming of something. The spirit of a coyote. She probably had something like that. The coyote is aware of people, but doesn't really mix with them. They say Chiwid used to shoot one coyote a year.

That's the way Chilcotin people pray. They dream like that. Some people use that for a good reason, some people don't. Chiwid never really prayed over someone to heal them, but she didn't hurt anybody either. She just used that power to stay outside.

Chiwid used to camp right beside my garden at Stone, and she used to help herself. When I came by she used to tell me she was growing her own vegetables. She said she was growing her own garden. I didn't care. She didn't eat that much anyways. The only way she ate was by helping herself. Other people used to give her groceries too.

ZALOWAY SETAH *and his wife, Katie Quilt, looked after Chiwid at Stone Reserve for the last few years of her life. They took her into their*

house after she became blind and was unable to look after herself.
This was the first time in more than 50 years that Chiwid actually
allowed herself to live indoors for any more than a few days at a time.

Chiwid wouldn't stay with people. There's very few people she
likes. Maybe she stays with us because she likes us. Maybe, I don't
know. Because she don't stay very long with other peoples.

Before she moved into our house, she lived on the reserve by herself a while. Charlie Quilt had a saw and cut her wood once in a
while. She usually just burned limbs and that.

She didn't have much around her camp. An axe, a butcher knife
maybe. A penknife maybe, just as long as you could cut with it.

She used to have lots of stuff before. Some of it she left behind.
She used to stay with her daughter at Tatla Lake.

Chiwid didn't tell much stories when she was staying with us. I
didn't ask anything and she didn't tell me about it. She never tell me a
story. I just never bother her.

She seemed happy staying with us. At least we don't bother her. We
leave her alone. That's the way she was living, I guess. Lay around
most of the time.

She stayed in the room by herself. She had to, because she was
blind when she was here. She couldn't go any place by herself
because she couldn't see. Unless you take her some place. It was different when she was young.

I never ask anybody what that name "Chiwid" means. That's the
way they call her. Most the time I call her Lillie Jack. That's her married name. I don't know if Chiwid means chickadee. Maybe that's
what it means. Well, that would be a tough bird. That's winter bird.
Yes, it could be that it means that.

ROSALIE DAWN HAINES *is one of Julianna Setah's younger daugh-*
ters, and a granddaughter of Chiwid. She spent a lot of time with
Chiwid during her last days.

Grannie used to call white people "Bostons." She said: "They don't come around for nothing – they always want something."

She used to say: "When all the coyotes died out, that's when I'm going to die."

HENRY SOLOMON *is a respected Tsilhqot'in elder. He lives in Nemiah Valley with Mabel, his wife.*

I guess one year it was 50 below. Chiwid still camp outside at Stone Reserve. Every time, somebody told him he's going to freeze outside. Chiwid, he don't want to stay inside. He say: "It's good to stay outside. More better. Cold wind. North wind."

Chiwid was kind of a witchdoctor. He dreamed of coyote. Coyote, he won't freeze. Chiwid, he dream about something like that. Kind of a witchdoctor. Suppose you not like that, you're going to freeze.

He don't have much blanket. Just sleep right under the blanket. Maybe put a little tarp over him. Every place he go, he don't put up no tent, nothing. So he do that all the time.

You know, when Chiwid sleep you don't know which way his head is. Just curl up like a coyote. Like a dog put his head under him like that. Just curl up like that. Chiwid sleep like that. I seen him. Just sleep there right out, open place. Maybe put a little tarp over. Sleep like that all winter. Snow on top. He don't care. Seem like he don't feel the cold at all. Got a little camp fire, that's all. Sit beside. About 20 below wind. Must be tough.

Sometime, Chiwid go way down to Riske Creek. Way down through the pass. Way down along the river. Pick them blackberries down there. Saskatoon trees grow real long, down along the river.

Chiwid he come from Tatla Lake, that country. He used to live all over. Anahim Lake.

So he go down there to Riske Creek. He just have a pack horse and one more horse. Chiwid and his daughter, Mary Jane, that was married to Henry Lulua. That little girl, that's the only one that ride a horse that time. Chiwid, he don't want to ride a horse. Just lead him. Pack the little girl. Chiwid, he just walked.

I was about eight years old when I first see Chiwid. I was raised at Toosey reserve by my grandmother.

Long time ago, lots of people they go pick berries at Riske Creek. They come from Redstone and Anaham. They go down with a wagon. Before there were hardly any cars. That time, Chiwid go down with a pack horse and pick some berries along the river down there. He camp by himself all the time. Seem he don't like to camp around pretty close to anybody. Seem like just that little girl go with him, and he camp some place. But he don't want to camp around a bunch of people.

That first time I see Chiwid, he looked pretty good. Strong. When he go down the river, it's a long ways down there. Maybe three miles. Real hot down there. Kind of rocks all over. The last time we went down there, me and my wife and her mother and old man Sammy, Mabel's dad. That time we see Chiwid picking some berries down there too. That must have been 30 years ago.

Once we were going to Anahim Lake. We go by the wagon through Tsuniah. Then we come out at Tatla Lake. Then, just on the other side of Tatla Lake, we found a junk pile there. We got no spare tire for our wagon, so we stopped to look for a tire. My wife, he look way over there and see somebody sitting over there. So we went over there. Chiwid was sitting right there. Got a bunch of stuff all over. Camp right there. He don't want no tent. He sleep under a tree.

His mind not very good, Chiwid. He told us somebody kill somebody. Somebody got knocked over the head. He said they take him back to Anahim Lake. We went over to Anahim Lake. Nobody got killed. Guess he just say that way.

One year, we see Chiwid coming along the road, way down by the bridge at Taseko River. See her coming this way. We were on our way home. Pick up our kids from the school bus at Stone Reserve. We see Chiwid packing her stuff alongside the road. So we stop.

We tell him: "We take your stuff to Tommy Lulua's place at Henry's Crossing?" He said: "Just past Tommy's place and then camp."

So we bring his stuff right out. Piled up his stuff before we left.

Pretty soon, Tommy, I guess he go and see Chiwid. Tommy Lulua, he told Chiwid: "We stay together?"

Old Chiwid, he say he don't want no more man no more. He told Tommy he don't like no man like you anyway. So, Chiwid don't want to go with him.

"Suppose you stay with me," Tommy Lulua tell him. "You not going to stay under the tree no more. You stay in good house."

He say he got lots of grub and stuff like that. He say he got lots of cattle.

Still, Chiwid, he don't want him Tommy. He told Tommy he don't want no more man. Can't stay with you. That's what he do. So Tommy, he don't bother Chiwid no more.

One time, I stay with Chiwid in the hospital. He was blind already. Got cold sick from staying outside. I got sick, too. So I stay in the hospital. I guess Chiwid got no Tsilhqot'in to talk to in the hospital, so that nurse want me to talk to him. I talk to him for a long time.

I ask him: "Which way you leave Alec Jack?" I told him.

He say: "One fellow, he fool me pretty bad."

So I tell him: "What you do?"

He tell me: "One fella just look like Alec Jack. He got his hair combed just like Alec Jack. He look like same as Alec Jack. That's the fellow that fool me."

Chiwid tell me he start to stay with that fellow for quite a while. Pretty soon, some way, he find out. He figured that fellow wasn't Alec Jack. So he said he left him again.

That's what he said. I guess he kind of went cuckoo. He said he don't want to get fooled anymore.

Alec Jack, he talk to you really good. Tell you lots of oldtimer story. He stay with me eight months. Every day he tell you different story. About a long time ago before any white people around here. Long time ago there's a bunch of Chinamen along the Fraser River.

Chiwid get pretty blind when he stay at Stone. One time we watch him shoot ducks. He can really shoot good. Every shot he got something. Right in front of Stone, way out in the field. We watch him. Pretty soon, he go way out there. Pick up the ducks and bring back to his camp. Pretty good shot.

Sometime, a witchdoctor can shoot. He can't miss nothing. Witchdoctor used to be like that before. Don't matter where he shoot, he kill them. I think Chiwid like that some way. That's why every shot he get something. Some kind of witchdoctor. Can't miss anything.

Seem like Chiwid don't stay with people. Long time ago, witchdoctor don't like to stay around with a bunch of people. Don't stay in a group. Some people like that before.

Dream like coyote all the time. Then you make some noise like a coyote.

ACKNOWLEDGEMENTS

I would like to thank two special friends, Liz Robertson and Diana French, for encouraging me to undertake this project.

Special thanks also to Julianna Setah and her daughter Rosalie Dawn Haines for giving me permission to research and write about their mother and grandmother.

This book could not have been written without the cooperation and enthusiasm of those individuals whose stories are contained in these pages. More than 80 individuals were interviewed, and I would like to acknowledge the following: Gladys Blatchford, Johnny Blatchford, Bill Bliss, Irene Bliss, Lee Butler, Alf Bracewell, Gerry Bracewell, Fred Brink, Leona Brink, Andy Cahoose, Susan Cahoose, Patrick Charlieboy, Tom Chignell, Eve Chignell, Mike Christensen, Frank Chundee, Elaine Dester, Mack Dester, Edna Dowling, Baptiste Elkins, Donald Ekks, Emily Ekks, Al Elsey, Julie Elsey, Alice

Engebretson, Fred Engebretson, Harold Engebretson, Don Fadenrecht, Illa
Graham, Joy Graham, Roy Graham, Josephine Gregg, Rosalie Dawn Haines,
Marie Hardy, Harry Haynes, Laurie Haynes, Lou Haynes, Wilf Hodgson,
Teresa Holte, Tommy Holte, Louisa Jeff, Bob Jenkins, Mildred Jenkins, Otto
Johnny, Grace Kellogg, Ollie Knoll, Hank Law, Dougan Leon, Casimile
Lulua, Doris Lulua, Madeline Lulua, Hugh MacDonald, Bud McLean, Alex
Matheson, Rita Meldrum, Marty Moore, Jane Mueller, Randolph Mulvahill,
Douglas Myers, Helena Myers, Carm Perjue, Willard Perjue, Charlie Quilt,
Catherine Robertson, Joyce Robertson, Phil Robertson, Josephine Robson, Jack
Ross, Mary Ann Ross, Ed Schuk, Helen Schuk, Joe Schuk, Katie Schuk, Alex
Seaforth, Doreen Seaforth, Julianna Setah, Zaloway Setah, Scotty Shields,
Edward Sill, Timothy Sill, Henry Solomon, Andrew Squinas, Helen Squinas,
Thomas Squinas, Lucy Sulin, Willie Sulin, Euphrasia William, Ev Wilson,
Gordon Wilson.

For the photographs used in this book, I'd like to thank Johnny Blatchford,
Veera Bonner, Al Elsey, Joy Graham, Marie Hardy, Harry Haynes, Laurie
Haynes, Lou Haynes, Wilf Hodgson, Henry Lulua, Helena Myers, Colleen
Salmon, Bernice Whitey, Euphrasia William, and Ev Wilson.

For financial support, thanks to the Canada Council Explorations Program, the Cariboo Friendship Society, and the Secretary of State, Department
of Canadian Heritage.

Many thanks to Terry Glavin, who did a masterful job of editing the vast
heap of raw materials that were left on his doorstep — and weaving a story out
of it. Thanks also to publisher Rolf Maurer for his co-operation and faith that
the storytellers of the Chilcotin could indeed tell their own tale.

NEW STAR BOOKS LTD.

107 – 3477 Commercial Street, Vancouver, BC V5N 4E8   CANADA
1574 Gulf Road, No. 1517, Point Roberts, WA 98281   USA
www.NewStarBooks.com   info@NewStarBooks.com

TRANSMONTANUS is edited by Terry Glavin. Editorial correspondence should be sent to 3813 Hobbs Street, Victoria, BC V8P 5C8
terry.glavin@gmail.com

Cover by Mutasis.com
Interior design by Val Speidel
Cover photo by Veera Bonner
Map by Fiona MacGregor
Printed & bound in Canada by Marquis Imprimeur Inc.
Printed on 100% post-consumer recycled paper
First published 1995. Reprinted 1998, 2009

The publisher acknowledges the financial support of the Government of Canada through the Canada Council for the Arts and the Department of Canadian Heritage Book Publishing Industry Development Program, and of the Province of British Columbia through the British Columbia Arts Council and the Book Publishing Tax Credit.

CANADIAN CATALOGUING IN PUBLICATION DATA

Birchwater, Sage.

  Chiwid

(Transmontanus, ISSN 1200-3336; 2)
ISBN 0-921586-39-6

  1. Chiwid 2. Chilcotin Indians — Biography. 3. Indians of North America — British Columbia — Williams Lake — Biography. I. Title. II. Series.

E99.T78C54 1995   971.1'75   C95-901616-2